P9-EEL-047

THE LIFE OF WINSTON CHURCHILL

Books for Children by Leonard Wibberley

NON-FICTION: The Life of Winston Churchill
The Epics of Everest
The Coronation Book

FICTION: The Wound of Peter Wayne
Deadmen's Cave
The Secret of the Hawk
The King's Beard

THE LIFE OF

Winston Churchill

By LEONARD WIBBERLEY

ARIEL BOOKS • *NEW YORK*

FARRAR, STRAUS AND CUDAHY, INC.

Ariel Books
is a division of
Farrar, Straus & Cudahy, Inc.

Published simultaneously in Canada by Ambassador Books, Ltd.,
Toronto. Manufactured in the U. S. A.

FOREWORD

When i was sixteen years of age, I was a copy boy on the *Sunday Dispatch* in London. One day I was sent to the waiting room where a visitor was waiting to see the editor, Charles Eade.

Editors were very big men indeed to me then; demigods who were not to be disturbed by people dropping in to see them without an appointment.

"What is your name?" I inquired of the visitor and added discouragingly, "the editor is very busy and I don't think he will be able to see you."

"My name is Winston Churchill," was the reply. "As for my business, I have an article to submit to him." That was my first contact with the man who later became Britain's wartime Prime Minister. At the time he was a very forlorn figure, a private member of Parliament warning against the rise of Hitler's Germany. Nobody would listen to him.

Many years later, as U.S. correspondent of the London *Evening News,* I again met Winston Churchill when he came to the United States to deliver the ad-

dress at Fulton, Missouri, when he coined the phrase "Iron Curtain." It was rumored that he would be given the position of Secretary General of the newly formed United Nations organization. My task was to find out whether he was to be Secretary General or not. Time and again I put the question to him at a hectic press conference on the Cunard dock in New York. Time and again he parried it by answering other questions instead.

Finally, seated only a few feet from the great man, I got his attention and asked once again whether he was to be Secretary General. He hesitated a second, and in the silence a society editor asked Winston how many cigars he smoked.

Delighted at getting out of a tight spot he replied cheerfully, "That depends on the length and thickness of the cigar." And so my question remained unanswered.

These are meager incidents with which to set out to write a biography of Churchill. I can claim no intimacy with him other than that which comes to a newspaper man of twenty years' practice. But the material on Churchill is so rich and so great that the problem has been not one of searching for incidents and anecdotes, but rather of eliminating and sifting them. In this process much of real interest has had to be left out. Yet I hope that in this life of Churchill for younger readers, I have attained a sufficiently balanced story to cover the main facts of his career.

It has been a great pleasure to write this book which was suggested by Jean P. Colby. I hope those who read it will get as much enjoyment as I did in writing it.

LEONARD WIBBERLEY

THE LIFE OF WINSTON CHURCHILL

CHAPTER

1

ON NOVEMBER 30th, 1874, a huge ball was being
held at Blenheim Palace, near Woodstock, England, the home of the Dukes of Marlborough. Prominent among the guests was Lord Randolph Churchill,
son of the seventh Duke of Marlborough and his Amer-
ican-born wife, Jennie. The family had tried to dis-
suade Lady Churchill from attending the ball because
she was expecting a child. But she was high spirited
and since her baby was not due for some weeks, insisted that she would be present.

When the festivities were at their highest, however,
Lady Churchill became faint and was taken quietly to
a cloakroom. There, amidst mounds of ladies' wraps
and feather boas, gentlemen's silk hats and opera
cloaks, Winston Leonard Spencer Churchill, who was
later to become twice Prime Minister of Great Britain

and one of the greatest men of the twentieth century, was born.

From his earliest days, Winston Churchill has surprised all who had any contact with him. Because of his premature birth, his parents believed that he was a sickly child. Certainly he was small, and his shoulders were stooped. His red hair formed a violent contrast with his somewhat pale face. He surprised everybody by becoming a first-class polo player and winning the British public schools fencing championship.

At school he could get nowhere with mathematics. Yet he became Chancellor of the Exchequer with the task of putting together the enormously complicated budget of Great Britain.

He could make little or no sense of Latin or Greek and never graduated from Harrow, the school to which he was sent as a boy. As a man he received dozens of honorary degrees from some of the world's leading universities, and professors and teachers in every field have listened humbly to his pronouncements. Yet he never went to a university.

Again, although he was trained as a cavalryman, his sympathies have always lain with the British navy and he was twice First Lord of the Admiralty. And at the height of his popularity when he had led Britain to victory in World War II, the British people threw him out of office as their Prime Minister.

Contradiction and surprise. These are the keystones of Winston Churchill's life. And some clue to the reasons for them may be found in his parents and his ancestry.

Churchill's father, Lord Randolph Churchill, was one of the most brilliant statesmen and politicians in Britain in the Nineteenth Century. But he threw a glittering career aside because he could not get his own way over a minor point, and died a heartbroken man. His mother, Jennie Jerome, was the daughter of Leonard W. Jerome, a prominent American businessman of the last century. Leonard Jerome early made a fortune on the Wall Street stock exchange, was owner of the New York *Times* at one time, and took such an interest in horse racing that he became known as the Father of the American Turf.

Winston Churchill, then, combines the spirit of American initiative with the traditions of the British nobility. An ancestor, the first Duke of Marlborough, was one of the most famous generals in British history. On his mother's side, an ancestor of Winston Churchill's was one of George Washington's lieutenants in the Revolutionary War. He has said of himself that he is fifty percent American and a hundred percent British.

When Churchill was born, his parents were living at Blenheim Palace with the seventh Duke of Marlborough, Churchill's grandfather. The palace had been donated to the first Duke of Marlborough, Churchill's ancestor, by the British parliament, in gratitude for his magnificent victory over the forces of France and Bavaria at Blenheim in 1704 in the War of the Spanish Succession. The seventh Duke, Churchill's grandfather, ran the palace as if it were a ship. Nobody was allowed to be idle. Each hour of the day had to be devoted to some occupation or other. All adults were required to read the newspapers thoroughly, and were questioned by the Duke on their contents each day. Churchill's mother complained that she had to work so hard at her music, painting, and reading, that sometimes she thought she was living in a school rather than in a palace.

Two years after Churchill was born, Disraeli, Prime Minister of Great Britain, appointed the seventh Duke of Marlborough Lord Lieutenant of Ireland. The whole family then moved to Dublin, and Winston Churchill's first recollections were not of Blenheim Palace with its huge rooms, its picture galleries, its massive furniture, and its priceless collections of statues and other works of art. Rather, he remembered "The Little Lodge" which was the name of the house in Dublin where his father took up residence. Lord Randolph accompanied the Duke to Dublin as an unpaid private secretary. The Duke lived in the Viceregal Lodge, an imposing building in grounds of its own, and "The Little Lodge" was situated a few hundred feet from this.

In Ireland Churchill showed himself a rebel from the start. He was, according to one of his nurses, the naughtiest child she had ever encountered. He had a very quick temper and strongly resented any discipline. Sentenced to go to the nursery for some piece of ill behavior, he would kick and scream so hard and so loud that his nurse, in the interests of peace, would have to give in to him.

Nurses could not stand Winston Churchill for very long, and rarely lasted more than a few weeks before quitting the job.

Eventually his parents engaged a very wise and understanding nurse named Mrs. Everest. She and Winston became close friends, so he quite often did what she asked of him. Mrs. Everest used to read him stories in the evenings and he loved adventure stories best. His favorite was Robert Louis Stevenson's *Treasure Island*. Pirates, mutinies, buried treasure, attacks on forts—that was the sort of stuff that appealed to young Churchill, and *Treasure Island* has remained one of his favorite books.

During World War II, when, as Prime Minister of Great Britain, the heaviest burdens were placed on him, Churchill once told his secretary that he was retiring to his study and must on no account be disturbed. Many urgent calls and callers were turned aside by the secretary until at last one caller came on such urgent business that the secretary felt he must disobey orders and interrupt Churchill. He knocked softly on the door and entered in great anxiety. And there was Churchill stretched out on a sofa, reading *Treasure Island* with the greatest enjoyment.

Some of Churchill's reactions as a boy would have disturbed a child psychologist. Once Mrs. Everest promised him that he would be taken to a pantomime in return for exceptionally good behavior. He was entranced at the prospect and looked forward for days to the event. However, when the day finally arrived, the building in which the pantomime was to be given burned to the ground before the doors were opened. The man responsible for the performance perished in the flames. All that was found of him were the keys to the building which he had had in his pocket.

Young Churchill was terribly disappointed at the news, and burst into tears. But he brightened up when told about the keys and horrified everybody by demanding that he be allowed to see them.

In 1880, when Churchill was six years old, Disraeli was defeated in a general election in Britain, and Mr. Gladstone, leader of the Liberal Party, who formed the opposition to the Conservatives, returned to power. The immediate effect upon Churchill was that his grandfather, the Duke of Marlborough, was replaced as Lord Lieutenant of Ireland, and the whole family moved back to England.

Churchill's mother was expecting another child—a brother John, who was born shortly afterwards. In the meantime Churchill was sent to Ventnor on the Isle of Wight in the English Channel with his nurse, Mrs. Everest.

This was a very happy experience for Winston, for Mrs. Everest's brother-in-law, who also lived at Ventnor, had been for thirty years the warden of a big English prison. He took Winston on many walks along the cliffs and told him stories of prison mutinies, attacks by prisoners and other exciting tales of personal adventure. He also discussed with him the details of the Zulu War which was raging at that time in South Africa. Churchill avidly soaked up details of attacks by huge black warriors armed with spears called *assegais*. His early years, then, were stocked with tales of adventure of all kinds, ranging from the pirates of Robert Louis Stevenson to prison riots and the African warriors. His toys reflected his interest in heroism and personal adventure.

Favorite among his playthings were toy soldiers. He started off with a small box of them and, encouraged by Mrs. Everest, eventually had a collection of a thousand. These included a division of infantry and a brigade of cavalry. It was while Churchill, scarcely seven, was fighting a mock battle with his toy soldiers in the family nursery that he made one of the greatest decisions of his life.

His father, Lord Randolph Churchill, passed by, and seeing the formidable array of soldiers on the nursery floor, and the considerable skill with which they had been laid out, asked Winston, "Would you like to go into the army when you grow up?"

Winston replied emphatically that he would.

So it was decided that Winston Churchill would become a soldier. Lord Randolph told a friend later that he made the decision thinking that his young son was not so very bright.

But first, the boy had to go to school. And Winston Churchill had already taken his stand on education. He would have as little to do with it as possible.

CHAPTER

2

WHEN HE WAS SIX, Mrs. Everest told her charge, Winston Churchill, that he was going to have to learn to read and do sums.

"Soon," she said, "you will have a governess who will teach you to read and add and subtract. But until she comes, I'll try to help you so it won't be so difficult."

Mrs. Everest had bought a book called *Reading Without Tears*.

"It certainly did not justify its title in my case," Churchill wrote of the book later. "We toiled each day. My nurse pointed with a pen at the different letters. I thought it all very tiresome."

Before he had gone very far with his first steps in reading, the governess arrived. Churchill promptly hid in the shrubbery in the garden and was not found for some time. Then his education commenced. Winston hated the whole business. It seemed a terrible waste of time which could be better spent playing with his toys or in the garden. Furthermore, he could make no sense of figures. He complained that they always got themselves tangled in knots. In subtraction they kept borrowing from each other and then had to pay each other back again, and it was very hard to keep the whole business straight. But the governess persevered, though Winston protested that sums were unfair. With anything else, he got some credit for being nearly right. But with addition and subtraction, being nearly right was no good at all. He was either completely right or completely wrong, and he thought this unreasonable.

The male Churchills had for generations gone to Eton, one of the great English schools. However, since it was mistakenly believed that Winston was a delicate child, his father and mother decided that he should go to Harrow. Harrow is located on a hill outside London, and it was thought that the higher elevation would benefit him. But first, he had to go to a preparatory school.

The one selected was St. James's School, which modelled itself upon Eton, and was very advanced, at least in its equipment, for its day. All the classrooms had electric light, which was quite unusual then, and there was a swimming pool, football and cricket grounds, and furthermore, the pupils were taken on a school treat three times each term.

All this suggested that the school would provide an ideal and kindly introduction to education for the sons of gentlemen. Winston's mother and father were hopeful that such a school would remove their young son's hostility to learning. But outward appearances were a mere disguise. The school was actually run with the harshest discipline, and from the time he went through its doors, Winston, though only seven, was in rebellion against it.

On his first day he was introduced to the master of his class who presented young Churchill with a book of Latin nouns.

"Memorize the different cases of the word 'mensa,' meaning 'table,' " the master said and departed. Churchill did not know what he meant. Before him was a list of words as follows: "Mensa. Mensa. Mensam. Mensae. Mensae. Mensa." The translations beside each word were of little help. One said "O table!"

When the master returned, Churchill had memorized the words, but did not understand them.

"What is the use of all this?" he asked. "What does 'O table' mean?"

"That is what you would say if you were talking to a table. You would say 'mensa,' meaning 'O table.' "

[13]

"But I never talk to tables," replied Churchill, "so it's all nonsense."

"Young man," said the master, "if you are imper-tinent, you will be punished, and very severely."

From that day forward Winston Churchill took a strong dislike to Latin. When he was introduced to Greek, he decided he did not like that language either. He would have as little as possible to do with them, and fear of punishment or failing examinations did not alter his attitude.

He got into a great deal of trouble at St. James's School. Partially the trouble arose from his own high spirits and rebellious attitude, partially from the sever-ity of masters who punished their charges with a can-ing for the slightest offense. The school had a punishment room to which the boys were sent for flog-ging. The caning however did not take place there, but in a small room adjoining. The wretched boys were compelled to sit with white faces listening to the cries of their schoolmates as they waited their own punish-ments.

Churchill was flogged frequently, perhaps more fre-quently than most of the pupils. The constant canings did not break his spirit and one day, according to his schoolmates, he got a measure of revenge by kicking the mortar board of one of the masters to pieces. That, of course, brought another flogging. Eventually his health suffered so badly that his parents decided to take him out of the school. Neither his father nor mother knew what had been happening to Winston at school, for all letters home were censored.

His next school was much less "modern" and much more kindly. It was run by two ladies at Brighton, on the south coast of England. Here Churchill was allowed to study things which interested him, among them French, history, and poetry. He also took lessons in riding and swimming, though he still would have nothing to do with either Latin or Greek. He regretted this in later life, but found a way of getting around his lack of Latin, as will be told.

When he was twelve, Winston Churchill was ready to take the entrance examination for Harrow. He was ready, however, only in the sense that he was old enough. He was an excellent reader and had a fair grasp of history and French. But his knowledge of two subjects was very slight. The first was mathematics and the second Latin. And, unfortunately, the entrance examination for Harrow demanded a good working knowledge of Latin.

The examination was conducted by the headmaster at that time, Dr. Welldon. Churchill, with the other candidates, was seated at a desk, given a pen and paper and some sheets of foolscap. Then Winston was presented with a series of simple sentences to be translated into Latin and other sentences to be translated from Latin into English.

"First things first," Churchill said to himself, and carefully put his name at the top of the paper. Then he placed the figure 1 neatly at the side. After some thought, he decided that this would make a better impression if he put brackets around it. So he did so, thus [1].

That, and a few blots and smudges which seemed to appear from nowhere, was the sum total of his results during the two hours of the examination.

When Dr. Welldon got his paper, he looked at it intently and then at the red-haired, blue-eyed, undersized boy before him. Then he sighed and made a decision which must have been based on nothing but pure intuition. Churchill never knew whether it was the brackets which he had placed around the figure 1, or the elegant way in which he had written his name at the top of the examination paper. But whatever the reason, Dr. Welldon decided to pass him, and so Churchill was admitted to Harrow.

Winston was, of course, put in the lowest division of the lowest form of the school. There were only two boys who were lower than he, and that was because their names were further down in the alphabet. These two boys left, and thus Winston Churchill became the lowest boy on the rolls of Harrow.

The passing of the years did little to improve his standing because of his inability to master either Latin or mathematics. But Churchill reaped one rich reward from his dislike of these two subjects. Boys at Harrow who were thought too stupid to learn Latin were given intensive instruction in English grammar and English literature. They drilled daily in analysis of English sentences, breaking them down into relative clauses, dependent clauses, adverbial clauses, and all their other varied parts. Churchill got three times as much instruction in English as the other pupils of his class because he remained in the class three times as long. His mastery of English, which served him so well later, arose from his being a duffer at Latin and mathematics.

Churchill never got into the upper classes at Harrow. He was always in the lower half of the school. Yet he did some surprising things.

Once he won a prize, open to the whole student body, for reciting twelve hundred lines of Macaulay's *Lays of Ancient Rome* without a single mistake. Such a feat of memory delighted and puzzled his masters. How could a boy memorize twelve hundred lines of verse and yet be defeated by the problem of learning a few rules of Latin grammar?

Again, Churchill passed the preliminary examinations for the army, although he was still at the bottom of the school. Boys far ahead of him failed these examinations. This success was probably due both to his huge toy soldier collection and the fact that the first Duke of Marlborough, one of England's greatest generals, was his ancestor.

Churchill admits that he was lucky in one respect in passing this army examination.

He knew that one of the problems would be to draw a map of some country. Other boys spent hours pouring over their atlases trying to remember towns, rivers, mountains, and shapes of coastlines and boundaries. Such a cautious approach was not for Winston Churchill. He put the names of all the principal countries in the world on pieces of paper and placed them in a hat. Then he shook them up vigorously and pulled out one. The name of the country was New Zealand, so he went dutifully to his atlas and, ignoring the rest of the world, memorized everything he could about New Zealand.

When he got the examination papers the following day, the very first problem was to draw a map of New Zealand.

Churchill's career now definitely pointed to the army, and he was placed in the Army Class at Harrow. His parents decided that, after leaving Harrow, Winston would go to Sandhurst, the British equivalent of West Point. But there was still the difficulty of mastering mathematics and Latin. Dr. Welldon, the headmaster at Harrow, went so far as to give Churchill private instruction in Latin. It did little good. For a while Churchill got by by writing essays in English for a boy who in return wrote Latin verses for Churchill. But this plan nearly came to grief, for the essays Churchill wrote were so good that the headmaster called the boy who submitted them and questioned him about them. The boy had a lot of difficulty in not revealing Churchill as the true author.

A thorough grounding in English, then, was Churchill's major achievement at Harrow. To it might be added an early lesson in diplomacy.

During the summer, the boys used to go swimming in a swimming pool so big that there were two bridges across it. It was a favorite pastime to push other boys, standing idly on the brim, into the pool. Churchill one day spotted a boy of his own size on the side of the pool, wrapped in a towel, and quite naturally crept up behind him, seized the boy's towel, and pushed him into the water.

He was horrified to find that the boy was the school gym champion, head of his house, and what would be called in America a football letter man. Churchill fled but was quickly seized by his victim and flung in the water in turn.

Later Churchill sought his victim out to apologize. His name was Amery.

[19]

"I'm sorry," Winston said. "I thought you were one of the lower school because you look so small."

This did nothing whatever to placate Amery, who didn't like being told that he was small. But Churchill made a brilliant recovery.

"My father, who is a small man too, is very famous," he said. Thereafter he and Amery were friends, and Amery later served in a number of cabinet posts in Churchill's government, including that of Secretary of State for India.

Churchill left Harrow without any distinctions other than winning the Headmaster's prize for memorizing poetry, and also winning, in 1892, the public school fencing championship.

At Harrow, despite his initial success, he failed to pass the entrance examination to the Royal Military College, or Sandhurst as it is popularly called. So he decided that he would "cram" for the examination with a private tutor after leaving school.

3

THE TUTOR selected to get Winston Churchill into Sandhurst was a Captain James who had a school in London which specialized in preparing students for the examinations. Captain James had a high reputation as a successful crammer, so much so that it was said of him that only a congenital idiot could fail to get into Sandhurst after being placed in his hands.

Winston Churchill, however, was very nearly killed before he got to Captain James' school.

At that time he was eighteen, and with his younger brother Jack, twelve, and a cousin, fourteen, went for a vacation to the estate of his aunt, Lady Wimborne, at Bournemouth. The estate was a wild place of perhaps forty acres. Through it ran a deep ravine which was spanned by a rustic bridge. Out of the ravine grew a number of pine trees whose tops nearly touched the bridge, thirty feet above.

Churchill organized a hunt in which he was the deer and the two younger boys the hounds. For some time he evaded them, but eventually they separated, and trapped him in the center of the bridge over the ravine.

With his brother at one end of the bridge and his cousin at the other, Churchill eyed the tops of the pine trees. Characteristically, the idea of surrender did not occur to him. He decided that it would be quite possible to jump to the top of one tree which seemed quite near, and tumble down through the branches safely to the ground.

He jumped, missed the tree, and fell to the bottom of the ravine.

It was three days before he recovered consciousness, three months before he could get out of bed, and a year before he could be pronounced recovered. His father, Lord Randolph Churchill, in Ireland at the time, rushed home and brought with him to Bournemouth the best surgeon available in England. Among other serious injuries, Churchill had ruptured a kidney. Only his own will to live and the skill of the surgeon pulled him through.

When he had recovered he was astonished and highly flattered at the expense to which his parents had gone to save him.

Not long afterwards, Churchill nearly lost his life

again. He had been sent by his father on a walking tour through Switzerland. Such tours formed an essential part of the education of English boys of wealthy parents in the last century. Little walking was done, but they had the opportunity to see at first hand how others lived, get a smattering of a foreign language, and climb a mountain. Churchill climbed two mountains and was disgusted that he could not climb the Matterhorn, thought to be the most dangerous ascent in Switzerland at the time.

One day he and a younger boy went for a row on Lake Lausanne. A mile off shore they decided it would be fun to go for a swim. Both stripped and dived overboard, exulting in the cold water. They did not watch the boat, which had a canvas awning on the stern. A slight breeze came up and the boat, with the awning acting as a sail, drifted away. When Churchill saw it, it was several hundred feet distant. He was a good swimmer and set out after it. But each time he approached, the wind would catch the awning again, and the boat would sail away.

Now he became frightened for the first time in his life. Death loomed plainly before him. He fought off a feeling of growing panic and started out for the boat again. Once more it drifted away when it was nearly close enough to grasp. Finally, almost exhausted, he reached the boat. A few more minutes and he and his companion would, without a doubt, have drowned. Churchill has never forgotten that experience.

Thanks to the heroic efforts of Captain James, and Churchill's own determination, Britain's future war leader finally passed the entrance examination for the Royal Military College at Sandhurst, but he barely got through. Because of his low grades, he was earmarked for the cavalry. Those who received higher marks always went into the infantry because it was less expensive. Not only were the uniforms cheaper, but it was not necessary to buy a horse. Churchill's father had already obtained a promise from a crack infantry regiment of a commission for his son when he left Sandhurst. Churchill was elated at going into the cavalry. He loved riding and was delighted at the prospect of owning a horse of his own.

But Lord Randolph was very angry. He wrote his son a stern letter about not studying hard enough, and added that while an officer in the infantry had to keep a personal soldier-servant (called a batman), in the cavalry he had to keep a batman and a horse as well. Little did Lord Randolph realize that one horse would not do. A cavalry officer had to have two official chargers, two hunters, and a string of polo ponies.

Churchill entered Sandhurst in 1894 and graduated with the commission of lieutenant eighteen months later. His attitude at Sandhurst was very different from that at Harrow and his earlier schools. He studied subjects which interested him, and pitched into the work with the zest he had previously reserved for resisting authority.

Mathematics and Latin he left behind for good. They formed no part of the teaching at Sandhurst. Later he found that an apt Latin quotation, delivered with authority, could be very helpful in parliamentary debates. Since he knew little or no Latin, he bought a book of quotations in that language, and memorized scores of them. The House of Commons many times applauded his scholarship, little realizing that its source lay in Churchill's astounding memory rather than familiarity with the classics.

The subjects of study at Sandhurst included Tactics, Map-making, Military Law, Fortifications, and Administration. Hours of study were long, but there were plenty of field exercises to delight Winston. These included instruction in blowing up railroad lines and bridges, making a primitive and unpredictable form of landmine, and drill afoot and on horseback.

Although he loved riding and horses, young Churchill was not a star at the beginning of his horsemanship at Sandhurst. Indeed, he was put in the awkward squad, and kept there until he improved.

He very much enjoyed his eighteen months at Sandhurst. His one complaint, shared by the other cadets, was that there seemed little prospect of a bang-up war breaking out. To be sure, there were a number of minor wars being fought in various parts of the British Empire against revolting tribesmen. But these were thought no real test of the courage and brilliance of a young officer and gentleman.

The fact was that the British army had not fought a war against a civilized power since the Crimean War, some forty years previous. The outlook for the professional soldier, hoping to put his skill to the test, was poor. Churchill and the other cadets at Sandhurst, clung, in their martial enthusiasm, to the faint hope that there might be a major revolution in India. In the meantime, they continued their studies.

Churchill's studies went so well that on leaving Sandhurst in December 1894, he was fourth in the riding school and graduated eighth out of a class of a hundred and fifty. He was now fully qualified for a commission in the army, and lacked only an appointment to a good cavalry regiment. But before his appointment came, his father died.

The tragedy was especially deep for Winston Churchill. A close friendship between father and son was rare in England in those days. The deep affection which existed between the two was kept hidden, for that was the style of the time, and showed itself only on rare occasions.

Churchill's father, Lord Randolph, had had a brilliant career. He was a man of genius, a gifted orator and debater. His foresight far exceeded that of many of his contemporaries. He had one fault, if indeed it could be called a fault. He would not be led, and would tolerate no opposition.

When Lord Randolph's party, the Conservatives, was out of favor, he was magnificent. Nothing so aroused his fighting spirit as defeat. This was a characteristic inherited by his son. But when the Conservatives were in power, Lord Randolph was a very difficult man to get on with. It was not that he was disloyal, but that he was an individualist, and would not part with his beliefs for the benefit of the party as a whole.

If he was opposed, his one answer was to resign whatever post he held. He was such an outstanding man and so thoroughly competent, that this was always sufficient. The opposition would be removed and Lord Randolph would return to his job.

But there came a day when he resigned once too often. A trivial question regarding the budget arose in which Lord Randolph's views were opposed to those of Lord Salisbury, the Conservative Prime Minister. Lord Randolph promptly resigned. To his surprise, Lord Salisbury quite as promptly accepted his resignation. His brilliant political career was over when he was only thirty-seven years of age.

Winston had from boyhood followed his father's political career with pride and a devouring interest. He read every speech his father made when it was printed in the papers. Occasionally he was present at luncheons and dinners in his father's house, when the guests were the greatest political figures in Britain of that day: Lord Balfour, Joseph Chamberlain, Edward Carson, Lord Rosebery, and many others. Sometimes he went to the Houses of Parliament to listen to his father debating on the floor of the Commons. All this bred in young Churchill a zest for politics which was second only to his enthusiasm for the army.

Once or twice during vacations Winston had offered to help his father's political work by letter writing, filing, and other secretarial services. He was always rebuffed. An English father of the Victorian era stood upon a pedestal. He did not share his work with his son.

Young Churchill, however, hoped that one day he might himself be in Parliament as a member with his father. They would have made a brilliant team. Lord Randolph's early death—he was only forty-five—ended that hope.

Winston Churchill would have to achieve whatever political career might lie ahead of him without his father's aid and advice.

CHAPTER

4

THE REGIMENT which Winston Churchill joined to start his career as a soldier was the Fourth Hussars. It was a very fashionable regiment with a dress uniform of dark blue larded with gold braid. Its commander, Colonel Brabazon, was an impoverished Irishman whose estates in Ireland provided him with very little revenue. He had entered the army to recoup his fortunes and was a fine soldier and a friend of the Prince of Wales.

Although the Fourth Hussars was a spit-and-polish regiment in the army phrase, it was also a famous fighting unit and the training and discipline of officers and men was of the hardest.

Winston soon discovered that despite all his instructions at the Royal Military College at Sandhurst, he did not know enough about riding to suit the Fourth Hussars. All young officers were sent for six months to the regimental riding school for intensive training in horsemanship. They trained with the troopers or private soldiers, and were treated exactly like them in every respect but one. That was, that being officers, they were expected to set a good example to the men with whom they trained. They must never show the slightest hesitation over any order, nor fail to report for duty because they had been hurt, unless the injury was very obvious and severe.

For six months Winston learned to mount and dismount from a barebacked horse at a trot and at a canter. He jumped his mount over high bars without the aid of saddle or stirrups and sometimes with his hands clasped behind his back. If the horse bungled the jump and crashed into the barrier, it was considered very bad form indeed for an officer to unclasp his hands before hitting the ground!

He fell so many times that he lost count. But always, whatever his bruises, he had to pick himself up with dignity, put his pill-box hat back on his head, and remount the animal. Once he tore a leg muscle. Though the injury was very painful, he could not ask to be excused from riding drill for a day or two until the muscle healed. That would mark him as a *booby* and he would lose the respect of the men. So he continued his training with the injured muscle, collecting a great many more falls before it healed.

The result of all this training was that Churchill became an excellent horseman.

Churchill at this time spent all he could on the purchase of polo ponies. Polo became a favorite, though expensive, recreation. He developed his own style, compounded of spirited, reckless dashes and much flailing of his polo stick. A friend said that Churchill playing polo reminded him of someone whacking away at a cobra with a whip.

At about this time Winston's old nurse, Mrs. Everest, fell ill. Churchill, hearing the news, obtained leave from his regiment, went to London, and engaged a specialist and two doctors to attend to her. He called on her in her house in North London. It had been raining and his old nurse, ignoring her own fatal illness, felt his jacket which was wet and would not rest until he had taken it off and it was dried.

Winston had to leave her bedside at midnight to get back to Aldershot, where his regiment was quartered, and take part in the morning parade. But as soon as this was over, he returned and was with Mrs. Everest in her final moments.

Winston Churchill never forgot Mrs. Everest and her great care and love for him. In his later years in Parliament, he worked hard for a program of pensions and health insurance for elderly folk, so that they would have money, if needed, and medical care in their final years.

Riding, polo playing, hunting and parade ground exercises were well enough, but they were not what Winston Churchill had joined the army for. He wanted to get into a war. He wanted to find out what it was like to be under fire, and take some part in real fighting. It was not that he was bloodthirsty, but rather that he was looking for excitement and adventure.

Churchill, after looking around for a war to get into, decided that it would be a good idea to go to Cuba, whose people in 1895 were in revolt against Spain. He suggested the trip to a brother officer, Reginald Barnes, who immediately fell in with the plan. Through a friend of his father's, Sir Henry Wolff, the British Ambassador at Madrid, the venture was arranged. Churchill and Barnes were given permission to go to Cuba and see what war was like at first hand.

Both found that, at least as far as the Cuban revolt was concerned, war was pretty dull. Before setting out, Churchill arranged with the London *Daily Graphic* to be their correspondent in Cuba, and so made his first appearance as a newspaperman and war correspondent. He was to be a war correspondent several times later, and the work did much to further his career.

In Cuba he was attached to a column of the Spanish government forces which was to penetrate into the interior of the island and wipe out the rebels. Unfortunately, it was very difficult to find them, and no pitched battles worthy of the name were fought. The Cuban rebels had organized themselves in guerilla parties. They would fire a few shots from the thick bush and then disappear. During one such sneak attack, a bullet whistled over Churchill's head and struck a horse standing nearby. At another time, bullets splattered in to a hut in which he was sleeping. Nobody, however, bothered to get up and investigate the shooting. Churchill noted that a stout Spanish officer was sleeping in a hammock which lay between him and the enemy fire. He concluded that the officer provided ample protection and went back to sleep.

When Winston returned to England, his regiment, to his delight, was ordered to India. Since the regiment was to be there for from twelve to fifteen years, all officers were given six months leave in which to saturate themselves in the pleasures of London society before their long exile. Lady Randolph Churchill arranged a variety of splendid entertainments for her son, Winston. He went to all the great homes of England as a guest, and, indeed, as a kinsman to many of the hosts. In those days, when class lines in England were very strongly drawn, most of the big families were related by marriage or blood one to the other.

Society figures were the leaders of the government in

England at that time. Their interests lay in horse racing and fox hunting as much as in politics. The Prime Minister, Lord Salisbury, never summoned his Cabinet when there was horse racing at Newmarket. Parliament always adjourned when the Derby was being run so that the members could witness it and bet on the race. No great crises faced the world, and gentlemen of leisure had time and money with which to put on splendid entertainments.

In his six months leave before going to India, Churchill met several influential people. One of the most important was Sir Bindon Blood, whose ancestor, Tom Blood, a soldier of fortune, had once attempted to steal the crown jewels of England. Sir Bindon might be called the "trouble shooter" for the British Empire in India. Whenever the fierce tribesmen who lived in the foothills of the Himalayas poured out of their mountain homes to raid the rich cities of the plains, it was Sir Bindon's job to drive them back again. Churchill got a promise that if there were any future trouble on the Indian frontier, Sir Bindon would let him take part in the fighting. A young officer of Churchill's time had to use all the influence he could to go on active service. Winston did not want to be a mere parade-ground officer.

Churchill had a serious accident the day he arrived in India. There was a heavy swell running when the

small boat in which he was being ferried ashore reached
Sassoon dock, Bombay harbor. In trying to land,
Churchill grasped an iron ring in the wall of the dock.
The boat dropped from beneath him and his whole
weight came upon his right arm, dislocating the shoulder. Winston paid little attention to the accident at the
time, and did not bother going to the regimental medical officer for treatment. Gradually, the joint slipped
back into place. But since then, Churchill's right shoulder has had an uncomfortable habit of becoming
dislocated. It very nearly came out of joint once in making a sweeping gesture during a recent speech in the
House of Commons. It would slip out of place while he
was playing polo, swimming, reaching for a book on a
high shelf, and so on. As a cavalryman it was especially
serious for him to have his sabre arm handicapped. Yet
the injury saved his life, as will be seen later.

The India of Churchill's time was Kipling's India.
It was a land of barbaric splendor and grinding poverty, of military pomp, of tiger shooting, polo playing,
pig sticking, and blinding heat; of religious fanaticism
and sporadic warfare on the Northwest Frontier.

Churchill threw much of his considerable energy
into polo playing. The game is one of the most expensive sports in the world, for each player must have a
string of ponies as part of his equipment. Winston
spent all his spare money on ponies, even borrowing

from local moneylenders at the rate of two percent per month to improve his stable.

When his regiment had been in India only a few weeks, the tournament for the Golconda Cup was played in Hyderabad. This was the most important polo event in southern India, and Churchill's Fourth Hussars, newly arrived, were hardly expected to do well in it.

To win the cup, a number of regiments competed in an elimination contest. As luck would have it, the Fourth Hussars found themselves facing the Golconda team, drawn from the bodyguard of the Nizam of Hyderabad. The Golcondas were considered far and away the best polo team in southern India. Everybody sympathized with the Hussars, green from England, where polo playing was not considered anything near as professional as in India.

"We will win," said Churchill, who was always at his best form when the odds were heavy against him.

At first it looked as though he was going to be notably wrong. Within a few minutes of the opening of the match, the Golcondas had scored three goals; the Hussars nothing. But then the tide changed, and the final score was Fourth Hussars—9; Golcondas—3.

Within the remaining days of the tournament, the Fourth Hussars, with Churchill flailing away in his cobra-killing style, went on to beat all their opponents and win the prized Golconda cup. Never before, in the history of Indian polo, had a regiment only a few weeks out from England achieved such a feat.

In the midday heat, when the sun was too fierce for any activity, Churchill spent his time educating himself.

This was a remarkable about-face for Winston Churchill who, since he had first been introduced to schooling, had put up a stiff and determined battle against education. But the difference was that now learning was a matter of his own choice. It was not undertaken at somebody else's order.

"What is meant by ethics?" he asked himself one day, and tried to reach an answer out of his own experience. Was it "playing the game"? Was it acting in an honorable manner, paying one's bills and not telling lies? Or was it something more than that?

He decided to find out and turned to the works of the great writers on the subject, among them Plato and Aristotle. These were the same works he had refused to study at Harrow. Now, in their English translations, he devoured them. Books whose very titles would previously have appalled him, he now read from cover to cover. Among them were Lecky's *Rise and Influence of Rationalism* and *History of European Morals,* Southey's *Colloquies on Society,* Artistotle's *Politics,* Gibbon's famed *Decline and Fall of the Roman Empire,* Dar-

[37]

win's *Origin of Species,* and the essays and histories of Macaulay.

All this intake of learning developed too much pressure to be kept within. Churchill had to give some of it out. His speech became richer, his style of writing more grand. He discovered that there was a certain fascination to talking (or rather orating) at length to his fellow officers, calling upon his new knowledge.

His fellow officers suffered for a while and then one said, "Next time young Churchill starts to let off a head of steam on ancient Rome or Darwin's monkeys, let's sit on him." The others agreed, and they had not long to wait.

One evening in the officers' mess, Churchill got the bit between his teeth on the subject of modern morals and went on for an hour with hardly a pause for breath. His listeners nodded to each other, Winston was seized, and thrust beneath a sofa. There he remained for the rest of the evening while his captors played several hands of bridge. Nor could he obtain his release with all the eloquence at his disposal.

But garrison life in India became monotonous, despite the fascination of polo and the hazards of lecturing in the officers' mess. Churchill applied for three months leave and returned to London looking for adventure.

CHAPTER

5

CHURCHILL WAS NOT very many days in England before he found what he wanted. While attending a race meeting at Goodwood, his eye caught a headline in a newspaper. It said that the Pathans had revolted on the northern frontier of India, and Sir Bindon Blood, with a field force of three brigades, was rushing to put down the insurrection.

That was enough for Winston. Here was a war—a real war. It was a little one, but likely to be sharp and dangerous. And Sir Bindon Blood had promised that he could go with him on his next expedition.

Winston dashed off a cable to Sir Bindon asking permission to join the expeditionary force and reminding him of his promise. He didn't wait for a reply, but caught the first train to Brindisi, where he would pick up a boat for India.

He hoped Sir Bindon's reply would be waiting for

him in Brindisi when he got there. It wasn't. The reply was not at Aden, in the Red Sea, where his ship stopped, either. But when he landed in Bombay a telegram from Sir Bindon was handed to him. It read: "Very difficult; no vacancies; come up as a correspondent; will try to fit you in."

To get into a war, Churchill, although a professional soldier, had to become a newspaper correspondent for the second time. Winston went to Allahabad where a newspaper, the *Pioneer,* was published, and persuaded the editor to appoint him as war correspondent. His mother, in London, had meanwhile tried to get him accredited to an English newspaper, and finally got him appointed correspondent for the campaign to the London *Daily Telegraph.*

This done, Churchill asked leave from the Colonel of his regiment and set out for the headquarters of the British force sent to subdue the Pathans.

"Give me a ticket to Nowshera," he told the Indian clerk at the railroad station, pushing a bag of rupees through the window.

The clerk gave him a pasteboard ticket. Churchill looked at it and said, "What? No change? How far is Nowshera?"

"It is two thousand and twenty-eight miles," replied the clerk politely. "Does the sahib require a return ticket?"

Churchill went back to his bungalow and picked up another sack of rupees for spending money on the five-day trip. He had no idea that India was so big.

When he arrived at Nowshera to join the Malakand Field Force—that was the name of the expedition sent to quell the Pathan rising—Winston found that Sir Bindon Blood had left to deal with a rising of the Bunerwals. This was a tribe living in a neighboring valley. He was away five days on this chore. Churchill, in the meantime, decided he had better fit himself out for the coming fighting, for he had arrived with little more than a couple of changes of clothing.

"It will be easy to get what you need here," an officer told him. "Several officers were killed in a skirmish the other day, and their gear is to be auctioned off."

Winston was able to buy boots, coat, water bottle, cooking pot, two horses, and engage a groom.

When Sir Bindon returned, the Malakand Field Force marched in three companies up the Mamund Valley to the seat of the revolt. Churchill joined the group which was to go to the furthest part of the valley. Theirs was the most difficult task, for the tribesmen around were hostile. Although farmers, they were also warriors. Every village was a fortress. It was not long before Churchill's group was being fired upon by the tribesmen, who were expert rifle shots.

The commanding officer decided to attack a fortress-village on the top of a hill at the end of the valley. He had only a few men (five officers and eighty-five Sikh soldiers), but there was a reserve of the Bengal Lancers and the Royal West Kent Regiment, which could be called upon for help. These remained for the time being in the valley below, but were to follow later.

The village could be reached by a ridge leading up from the valley, and the little company started climbing up this. They arrived at the village to find it deserted. They also found that they were cut off, for the reserve force, for some reason, had failed to follow them. A few hundred yards away, on the mountainside, were several hundred Pathans. The obvious thing to do was withdraw.

But no sooner had the British force started to retreat than the Pathans launched an attack. The mountainside was suddenly alive with them. They dropped down the steep sides like monkeys, their swords flashing in the bright sunlight. Their skill was amazing. They took leaps of twenty and thirty feet from crags and landed unhurt on the steep mountain slope. By this time most of the British force had left the village, and Churchill, who had remained behind with the rearguard, became aware that with less than a dozen men he faced several hundred warriors.

Up to this point he had been taking a few notes in a notebook. Now he realized that, for the time being at least, the sword was likely to be mightier than the pen.

"Give me your rifle," he ordered a Sikh soldier near to him. The soldier obliged and Churchill, standing up, quite careless of the bullets that whined and hummed around him, carefully emptied the magazine into the hillmen.

When he turned around for more ammunition, he was surprised to find that three of his little group were writhing on the ground seriously wounded and two others were dead. Among the wounded was the only other British officer, whose face was a mass of blood, for his eye had been cut out by a bullet.

It was an unbreakable rule that no wounded men were ever to be allowed to fall into the hands of the tribesmen, who delighted in torturing all their prisoners to death, wounded or not. Luckily, some of the British force who had already retreated, returned to help carry the wounded men down the hill. Among those who came back to help was the Battalion Adjutant. Seconds later, the adjutant was himself shot. Four of his men grabbed him by his arms and legs and hustled him down the hill. But they had gone no more than a few paces when half a dozen Pathans suddenly rushed out of a house in the village, and charged. The soldiers dropped the wounded man and ran. The adjutant was sliced to pieces by the sword of the leading Pathan.

[43]

This was too much for Winston. With a loud cry he drew his cavalry sword and rushed at the man to avenge the death of his brother officer. He had won the public school fencing championship and was sure he could deal with a wild Pathan. But the other five Pathans came to the help of their leader, and Churchill decided he could not take on six opponents at once.

So he pulled out his revolver and, taking careful aim, shot the first Pathan. Then he looked behind him for a second and found himself alone. Not a single British soldier was in sight and other tribesmen were coming up fast. He fired a few more shots and then bolted down the hill, with the Pathans behind him, until he reached the rest of his company.

These were in a very poor way. No reserves had come to their help, and they had three quarters of a mile to go to reach the plain below. On either side were tribesmen, firing away as fast as they could. Churchill grabbed a rifle and started shooting. He remembered to take careful aim with each shot. This, of course, involved standing still, presenting an excellent target himself. He got off thirty or forty rounds with good effect while the wounded were slowly carried down.

At the bottom of the ridge the company re-formed. The Pathans almost encircled them and outnumbered them eight to one. The Colonel turned to Churchill.

"The reserves are only half a mile away," he said.

"Get through to them and tell them if they do not come immediately, we will be wiped out."

Churchill's mind worked fast. He did not want to be the sole survivor of a group of British soldiers slaughtered by tribesmen on the Northwest Frontier. If there was going to be a slaughter, he would prefer to be among the victims.

"You'll have to put that order in writing, sir," he said.

The Colonel looked at him in amazement and fumbled in a breast pocket for notebook and pencil. Meanwhile, a captain had managed to restore the morale of the outnumbered Sikhs. "Volley firing," he shouted. "Ready! Present! Fire!" The rifles rattled in unison and a hole appeared in the packed mass of the Pathans. Two more volleys and they wavered. As the fourth volley crackled over the hot plain, a bugle shrilled the "charge" from the rear. Reinforcements had arrived at last, and the Pathans fled back to the mountains.

That, however, was not the last of the action. The body of the adjutant still lay on the ridge and had to be recovered. So the ridge had to be retaken, which took several hours of hard fighting. But Churchill came through without a scratch.

The next two weeks were spent in laying waste to the Mamund Valley in retaliation. Houses were destroyed, wells filled in, fortified towers blown up and crops burned. It was harsh punishment for the tribes-men, but the only way they could be subdued.

Churchill won several honors from the campaign. He was mentioned in dispatches for his part in the battle on the ridge. His reports to the *Daily Telegraph* were avidly read and made his reputation as a war correspondent. And he wrote a book about the whole expedition called *The Story of the Malakand Field Force.* This was a great success, and brought him a letter from the Prince of Wales, afterwards King Edward VII.

His Royal Highness, who had met Churchill at several functions in London, wrote:

"My dear Winston:

"I cannot resist writing a few lines to congratulate you on the success of your book! I have read it with the greatest possible interest and I think the descriptions and the language generally excellent. Everybody is reading it, and I only hear it spoken of with praise. . . ." The letter went on to express the hope that Churchill would remain in the army (and perhaps win a Victoria Cross), rather than branch off into politics.

To that date, Churchill had shown a keen interest in politics, but mostly as a spectator. The fears of the Prince of Wales, that Winston might enter politics, were well founded, though Churchill had not had his fill of soldiering yet.

CHAPTER

6

BOTH SIDES CLAIMED the victory after the battle of
the Malakand Field Force against the Pathans.
The British newspapers reported that the trouble on
the Northwest Frontier had been efficiently dealt with.
The Pathans rejoiced in the number of British soldiers
and officers they had killed and said they had won. A
little more effort, they were sure, and the British could
be swept out of the northwest portion of India and the
tribesmen would be able to loot the rich plains below
their mountain homes.

The Pathans persuaded the Afridis to revolt. The
Afridis are a very powerful tribe living around an area
called Tirah on the Northwest Frontier of India.
Churchill, ever looking for excitement, hoped that he
would be able to get into that war also, and for a while
it looked as though he might succeed. But eventually
the revolt petered out, and Winston was recalled to his

[47]

old command, the Fourth Hussars, still stationed at Bangalore two thousand miles away.

For some months he had to be content with the regular round of occupation duties—drill, inspections, polo matches, military receptions and so on. His fellow officers in the Fourth Hussars were for the most part friendly. But a number of them were a little jealous of the young second lieutenant who seemed to be able to get into any war that was going, and who combined the duties of a professional soldier with those of a war correspondent.

Churchill came in for some hostility from higher-ups after the publication of his book, *The Story of the Malakand Field Force*, for in it he had made some criticisms of the Army organization. Words like "medal-hunter" and "self-advertiser" were applied to him, though not in his hearing. This criticism came at an unfortunate time. For just after the Afridis campaign petered out, came news of a war against the dervishes in the Sudan.

The Sudan is a vast area, largely desert, which lies to the south of Egypt. The word is Arabic, meaning "black," for the people of the Sudan are among the darkest-skinned in the world. They are also among the fiercest. At the time, the Sudanese were led by one Abdullah el Ta'aisha who had proclaimed himself the *Mahdi* (or leader) of Islam. Most of the Sudanese are

Mohammedans and intensely religious, and Abdullah, who held the title of Khalifa, was a man of the cruelest nature into the bargain.

The British had a long grievance against the Sudanese because of the assassination of General C. G. Gordon at Khartoum some years previously. His death had gone unavenged, but now the Sudanese had risen against Egypt and Britain, and the time to avenge Gordon's death was at hand. The war promised every kind of military adventure and excitement, and Churchill was determined that he would be in the thick of it.

Now, however, he ran into determined opposition. Though he pulled every string he could, and had his mother use all her influence with her many high-placed friends and acquaintances, Churchill's application for a transfer to the war in the Sudan was turned down.

He learned that the opposition came from the highest authority—none other than Sir Herbert Kitchener who, as Sirdar, or commander in chief, of the Egyptian Army was in complete control of the field forces. Not even the British War Office could appoint an officer to serve on the front without his approval.

But Churchill is always at his best in adverse circumstances. He applied for leave to return to England, and, following his recent exploits on the Northwest Frontier, this was granted to him.

[49]

Back in London he buttonholed all the highly placed officers he could, trying to get into the Sudanese war. But it was no use. Kitchener had taken a firm stand. In no circumstances would he let the young and uppish son of the late Lord Randolph Churchill join his army.

Churchill's luck, however, had not deserted him. One day he received a letter which bore the exciting address "10 Downing Street, Westminster." That was the official residence of the Prime Minister, Lord Salisbury, in whose cabinet Churchill's father had served. The letter, from the Prime Minister's secretary, said that Lord Salisbury had read Churchill's book, *The Story of the Malakand Field Force,* and was intensely interested in it. He would like to meet the author and ask him some questions about the expedition. Could Mr. Churchill arrange to visit the Prime Minister at the Foreign Office?

Churchill quickly replied that he could, and soon he was discussing his book with Lord Salisbury. The Prime Minister spoke highly of Churchill's father and said he had learned more of the frontier war from Winston's book than he had through all the debates on the subject in the Houses of Parliament. In parting, he said that if there was any way he could assist Churchill, he would be glad to do so.

But so great was the power of Kitchener, that, even when the Prime Minister asked that Churchill be added to the officers in his army, Kitchener replied, "No." Churchill tried again. Kitchener undoubtedly had authority over the Egyptian army as Sirdar or commander in chief. But the British forces fighting side by side with the Egyptians was surely another matter. Churchill now worked through the Adjutant General of the British forces and was rewarded with an appointment to the 21st Lancers. His orders were among the strangest issued to any officer going to war. He was first of all appointed a supernumerary, or "extra" lieutenant, in the Lancers. He was to go to the Abassiyeh Barracks in Cairo, Egypt, the regimental headquarters. He was to pay his own passage, and if he were killed or wounded, no pension would be payable by the British Army.

Churchill didn't mind. To be sure, he had again to pay to get into a war, although a professional soldier. But he would see some real fighting, and that was what interested him.

CHAPTER

7

WINSTON CHURCHILL, who has perhaps made more money by writing than any man of his time, has never been one to pass up a business opportunity. Faced with the prospect of paying his own expenses in the Sudanese war, he went around to a friend of his, Oliver Borthwick, son of the owner of the *Morning Post*.

"Ollie," he said, "I'm going to the Sudan to join Kitchener's Army. How about a job as *Post* correspondent?"

"Would ten pounds (about forty dollars) a column satisfy you?" asked Oliver.

"Twenty would be better," replied Winston.

They settled for fifteen pounds a column, and Churchill was on his way with the *Morning Post* paying his expenses.

He arrived at headquarters in Cairo to find all seething with excitement. The 21st Lancers were just about to leave for the front. Two squadrons had left the day previously and two more were to leave upon the morrow. Winston was to have commanded a troop in one of these squadrons. But since until the last moment nobody was quite sure that Churchill would turn up, the command was given to another young officer, Robert Grenfell. Grenfell wrote home excitedly, "Fancy how lucky I am. Here I have got the troop that would have been Winston's and we are to be the first to start (for the front)." But Churchill's fabulous luck had not deserted him, even in this seeming reverse. Grenfell's squadron was cut to ribbons in the battle of Omdurman which followed, and Grenfell himself killed. Had Churchill been leading the squadron, he would assuredly have been slaughtered.

The journey up the Nile for the showdown battle with the forces of the Khalifa was colorful and exciting. There are a number of cataracts or rapids across the Nile through which the stern wheel steamships carrying Kitchener's army could not pass. Whenever a cataract was encountered, the whole force had to land, march along the shore past the cataract, and then reembark in other vessels. Each steamship pulled a tow of barges and dhows laden with supplies of all kinds from howitzers to hay. The heat of the day was intense. Soldiers wore felt pads over their spines to protect them from sunstroke, but many fell victim. Out on the blazing desert, mirage after mirage appeared and disappeared. At times a company of men would be seen marching across the desert apparently knee deep in water. They would approach so close that their banners could be almost distinguished. Then in a second they would disappear—another mirage.

Finally the whole force disembarked for the last stages of the advance on Omdurman where it was reported the forces of the Khalifa were drawn up. Churchill was sent to scout in advance and observe the enemy. A report had come in that the Army of the Khalifa was ahead and advancing.

"See the situation for yourself and then go back as quickly as you can without exhausting your horse and report personally to the Sirdar," his commanding officer said. "You will find him marching with the infantry."

This was the one thing that Churchill didn't want to do. He didn't mind getting close to the Khalifa's army and making an estimate of its number and disposition, though that could be dangerous. But he didn't like the idea of making a report to the Sirdar, Sir Herbert Kitchener, who had many times refused his application to join the army. Churchill feared that Kitchener might be angry and order him to the rear, where he would miss all the excitement.

But orders were orders and off he went. He found the Khalifa's army stretched out on a wide front and advancing. He estimated the number at forty thousand men, well armed, with several squadrons of cavalry. They were drawn up in good battle array. Then Churchill turned back to report to Kitchener, expecting the commander in chief would order him to the rear when he had made his report.

Winston found Kitchener riding a few paces ahead of the infantry columns. He made an imposing figure, sitting erect on his horse in the blazing sun with his two standard-bearers behind him. Every piece of his equipment glittered, from the banks of medals on his chest to the tips of his spurs. Churchill rode in from an angle, made a semicircle behind Kitchener and drew his horse alongside and to the rear of him.

Kitchener turned round to look at the young lieutenant. The Sirdar's cheeks hung down in jowls which had a purplish tinge. His eyes were big and bold and he wore a heavy walrus mustache. He looked exceedingly fierce.

Churchill saluted and said, "I've come from the 21st Lancers with a report on the enemy."

Kitchener nodded gravely.

"Proceed," he said.

Churchill told him all he had seen of the Khalifa's army while the commander in chief listened without an indication of what he was thinking or a sign that he recognized Churchill. When Winston had finished, Kitchener said, "You say the enemy are advancing. How long have I got?"

Churchill thought fast. The Khalifa's army had been about seven miles away and moving forward at perhaps four miles an hour. "About an hour, sir," he replied. "Perhaps an hour and a half."

Now, Churchill thought, it will come. Kitchener will send me to the rear for my impertinence in joining his Army against his wishes.

But instead, Kitchener merely bowed politely in his saddle, acknowledging the report and dismissing Churchill with the one movement.

The battle, which was expected in ninety minutes at the latest, did not, however, take place that day. The Khalifa halted his men in the desert and settled down for the night.

It was a night of great anxiety for the British army, especially the 21st Lancers. They were in the forward area and had been instructed on pain of death that no weapons were to be fired even if they were attacked. The cavalry would defend themselves with swords and lances, but were not to use guns. It was feared that in the tenseness of the night, a sudden burst of rifle fire might panic the army, the men would start firing without orders at unseen targets, and kill more of themselves than the enemy. This had actually happened some years previously in the Sudan when two Egyptian armies, meeting in the dark, had fought a pitched battle among themselves without one of the real enemy being killed.

The infantry brigades erected thorn barricades called zeribas for their protection against the dervishes of the Khalifa's army. The dervishes were experts at sneaking into the enemy's lines in the dark and cutting off people's heads.

When dawn came, Churchill was sent forward with half a dozen troopers to report on the enemy position. He found the Khalifa's army had grown remarkably during the night. Now, instead of forty thousand, there were sixty thousand. As the dawn light filtered across the desert, weaving strange shapes out of sandhills, rocks and valleys, he saw this huge horde advancing over the sands. They came like an irresistible tide. A thousand garish banners in brilliant colors floated over their heads, and from their ranks came a roar not unlike the approach of the ocean in flood. The troops of the Khalifa were cheering for God, for Mohammed his Prophet, and for the Holy Khalifa whose mission it was to wipe out the Christian infidels.

"Ul ul ul Akbar," came the cry from the approaching horde. Churchill was immensely excited at the sight. He rode forward about four hundred yards to a

hilltop to get a better view. He had already sent a mes-
senger back to Kitchener reporting that the dervish
army was on the move. This man now came back with
orders to remain and keep sending in reports of the
enemy.

Churchill was delighted. He had what amounted to
a grandstand seat from which he could see both armies.
Over towards the Nile, the British and Egyptian forces
were drawn up with their backs to the river. Behind
them were the gunboats which would soon open fire on
the enemy. On the other side, the Khalifa's men were
getting in battle formation. Churchill, on his hilltop,
was within two hundred yards of their outposts. A division of six thousand of the Khalifa's men massed themselves on a ridge nearby in plain view.

Suddenly the gunboats on the river opened fire. A
heavy rustling of shells rumbled over Churchill's head
and bigs gaps appeared in the massed ranks of the Khalifa's army. The enemy was so close that Churchill and
his men formed an unwitting part of the British target.
He saw the dervish warriors falling in shapeless masses,
but the horde still advanced down onto the plain toward the British zeribas. The dervishes fired as they
advanced and there was not the slightest hesitation
among them.

Blast after blast of artillery fire struck this moving
wall of men, ripping holes in it, but still it pressed for-

ward. Then a patrol of the Khalifa's cavalry headed toward the hill on which Churchill was posted. They carried long spears and wore heavy cowls like medieval monks. Churchill opened fire when they were within pistol range and they sheered off. Then a rider came dashing out of the British lines towards him, with orders to return as the infantry was about to open fire.

Churchill relinquished his grandstand seat at the battle, dangerous though it was, with reluctance.

The British and Egyptian armies numbered twenty thousand men, but they had the advantage of discipline and modern weapons on their side. They had soon stopped the dervish attack and Kitchener decided to advance on Omdurman, the dervish capital. He ordered the 21st Lancers to leave the thorn zeriba and reconnoitre the area towards the city.

The Lancers cheered. So far they had not struck a blow. Now, if things went well, they would have the fun of a real cavalry charge for which every one of them had been training for years.

Nor were they disappointed. Churchill on a gray polo pony, which he preferred to a heavier charger, was in command of a troop of twenty-five men. A division of dervish infantry had been drawn up in a shallow dried-up watercourse directly on the road to Omdurman. They opened fire as the Lancers approached and several horsemen and riders tumbled to the ground.

Then the bugler sounded the charge. The troops of cavalry wheeled into line. Lances were brought down to the ready, and to the jingle of harness the Lancers moved forward. Gradually the trot developed into a canter, and then into a full gallop.

Cries of "ul ul ul akbar" from the dervishes were answered by Harrovian football shouts from the British. Churchill, being a hussar, had a sabre rather than a lance. As he neared the enemy he suddenly realized that, because of his injured shoulder, he could not use it. He sheathed the sabre at full gallop and pulled out a German Mauser pistol which he had bought in London. A second later and his polo pony had leaped into the dried watercourse and he was surrounded by the dervishes.

Winston caught a glimpse of two black figures who leaped up before him. Both fired simultaneously at him, but missed. The trooper behind him fell dead. Churchill was now in a mob of screaming fighting warriors, armed with spears, guns and four-foot swords. Men and horses struggled and writhed in the ditch. The dervish tactics were to lie on the ground, hamstring the horses with their swords, and then cut the riders to pieces. Churchill somehow got through this mob to the other side of the ditch and paused to reload his pistol.

A dervish flung himself directly before his horse.

[61]

Churchill thought the man terrified until he saw him bring up his sword to hamstring the pony. He pulled the animal quickly aside and shot the man. As he started to rise he found a dervish horseman above him, his sword raised to cut off his head. Churchill shot him at such close quarters that his pistol actually struck the man. Churchill undoubtedly owed his life in this action to his dislocated arm. Had he been using a sabre instead of a pistol, he could not have dealt with two attacks in the space of one minute.

By now most of the Lancers had broken through the dervish line and were reforming to charge back again. Churchill joined them. Then right in the middle of the cavalry a dervish arose from the ground. How he got there, nobody knows. He charged at Churchill with a spear, and Winston shot him when he was only a yard or so away.

Then he turned to the sergeant of his troop.

"Enjoying yourself?" he asked.

"I'll enjoy it more when I get used to it," the sergeant replied.

Some of the wounded British now struggled out of the mass of the dervishes who were still in the ditch. They were an awful sight. Men with fishhook spears through them floundered across the desert. Some with limbs hacked off, and bleeding copiously, tried to drag themselves along the sand to safety. Horses hopped around on three legs whinnying in panic. But there was no time to attend to these casualties. The Lancers returned again to the attack, but this time tackled the ditch from both ends, catching the dervishes in such a hot fire that they scattered.

The charge of the 21st Lancers at Omdurman was one of the last major cavalry actions in western warfare. The Maxim gun and the machine gun abolished cavalry charges in the wars which lay ahead. Churchill is one of the few men living to have taken a part in such a charge.

He had come through the action without a scratch, but he did not leave Egypt without a reminder of the campaign. A fellow officer, Dick Molyneux, had sustained a sword cut above his right wrist which had severed all the muscles. His life had been saved by two of his troopers. Churchill met Molyneux on a sailing vessel which was taking them both down the Nile on the first stage of the trip back to England.

They chatted for a while and then the doctor came in to dress Molyneux's wound. The gash was huge and the doctor decided that an immediate skin graft was needed if the arm was to be saved.

He turned to the nurse and muttered something. The nurse bared her arm and her face went white. The doctor looked at her and then at Churchill.

[63]

"I'll have to take it off of you," he said. "Roll up your sleeve."

Churchill clamped a cigar in his mouth and bared his arm. The doctor took out a straight-edged razor, sterilized it, and carefully sliced a section lump of skin with an underlayer of flesh off Churchill's forearm to graft onto Molyneux's wound.

Winston Churchill still bears the scar today—a life-long memento of the charge of the 21st Lancers at Omdurman.

CHAPTER

AFTER THE SUDAN CAMPAIGN, Winston Churchill
returned to London to do some hard thinking.
He faced a crisis in his life which was summed up in
the question: should he remain in the army or should
he retire to civilian life and enter politics?

What brought the question to a head was the matter
of money. His mother had a modest income and property sufficient to keep her in good circumstances for the
rest of her life. But though he loved the army life,
Churchill found it a very expensive profession. His
officer's pay was small, and his officer's uniforms and
other trappings were expensive. He found that working for newspapers he had made quite as much money
as he had as a professional soldier. His book on the
Malakand expedition had brought in a nice sum and
he had written a novel, *Savrola,* which also sold well.

Dearly as he would like to continue in the army,

Churchill decided that he could not afford to do so. In view of the fact that he had had to pay his own expenses to get into the two wars in which he had fought, this was not a surprising decision.

After talking the situation over with his mother, he resolved to spend one more year as a soldier and then resign his commission. In civilian life he would support himself out of writing and would enter politics. This was the first time that Churchill had seriously considered entering the political field. It was an historic decision not only for himself but for the British people. If Queen Victoria had paid her officers better, it is quite possible that Winston Churchill would have remained in the army for life, and a brilliant statesman would have been lost to the world.

Winston's reason for deciding to serve another year in the army was typical of the man. The annual polo tournament was to be played at Meerut. His regiment, the Fourth Hussars, had a faint hope of winning it. Churchill was an important member of the team and rather than let his side down, he went back to India to play in the finals.

Shortly before the critical match, however, Churchill fell and dislocated his shoulder. He snapped the joint back into place himself (he had become quite expert at this). But he knew from experience that it would take three weeks before the muscles and ligaments recovered from the shock of the dislocation. And the polo tournament was to begin in three days.

"You must drop me immediately from the team," he told the captain, "for I will be quite useless. To win the tournament we need players in the best physical condition."

His teammates consulted among themselves and decided that Churchill would have to play.

"But I can hardly lift a polo stick, let alone hit a ball with it," Churchill said.

"You've more experience in the game than any of us," was the reply, "and even if you can't hit the ball, you'll be able to direct us and hold us together better than anyone else."

So Churchill, with his elbow strapped to his side, mounted his polo pony as a member of the Fourth Hussars team. In the first two matches, he confined himself to blocking the opponents for the team's top scorer, and the Hussars won. Then came the final match for the tournament cup. It was to be played against the Fourth Dragoon Guards, who were to polo in India what the Yankees are to baseball in America.

Churchill, finding himself in adversity with the odds against him because of his crippled right arm, rose magnificently to the occasion as always. He was no longer content with just blocking to let others score. Even with his elbow strapped to his side, he determined to do what scoring he could himself. When the match ended, the Hussars had won, and Churchill had scored three of the winning goals.

Then, after a farewell dinner with his regiment, he returned to England, to write and enter politics.

On his way from India he spent two weeks in Cairo, researching for a book which he planned to write on the Sudan campaign. He called it *The River War*. He increased its scope so as to give a great deal of the background of the British in Egypt and the Sudan. When published in two volumes, it became the authoritative work on the history of the British in those parts.

Churchill, as usual, did not pull any punches in writing, and Kitchener came in for some criticism from his pen. Churchill, while not directly blaming Kitchener, deplored the fact that at the battle of Omdurman, the British troops were left with the impression that the fewer prisoners taken, the better. He also denounced the razing of the tomb of the Mahdi in Omdurman. The Mahdi was the original leader of the Sudan revolt and had died some time before the battle of Omdurman, handing his authority on to the Khalifa. His tomb was sacred to the Sudanese, but it was utterly destroyed, the body dragged out, the head severed and carried about in a kerosene can as a trophy.

"Such was the chivalry of the conquerors," wrote Churchill in high indignation.

The two volumes had an immense sale and well rewarded the year they took to write.

When Churchill arrived back in England, he was invited to a great number of gatherings of soldiers, politicians, and financiers, for he was a well-known personality. It certainly seemed that it would not be at all difficult for him to win a seat in Parliament when a vacancy occurred. His father's brilliant record in Parliament and the Cabinet was still alive in the public memory. Churchill himself was one of the most decorated officers in the army. Further, he was an outstanding war correspondent and well-known an as author.

Winston threw himself into the task of getting into Parliament with all the energy he had put into fighting the dervishes of the Sudan and the Pathans of the Northwest Frontier.

But he quickly found politics a different kind of battle. The forces in opposition were not plainly in view. A swift decisive charge would not scatter them. An attack on the opposition in a speech might readily rebound, and one poorly selected word might doom a candidate at the polls.

Churchill belonged naturally to the Conservative Party. It was the party of his father, Lord Randolph, though Lord Randolph had had frequent disagreements with party leaders which had eventually led to his stepping out of political life.

The Conservatives, or Tories, as they are called, were the party of the business section of England. They believed in a firm hand overseas and the protection of British industry by tariffs and other devices. The opposition were the Liberals. Broadly, they stood for free trade and were opposed to the use of arms. They might be described as pacifist.

One day, Robert Ascroft, Conservative member of Parliament for Oldham, in Lancashire, invited Churchill to lunch with him at the House of Commons. The city of Oldham returned two men to Parliament both of whom were Conservatives at that time. One of these, however, was ill and expected to resign. Ascroft wished to know whether Churchill would like to contest the seat.

Churchill was elated at such a fine chance to enter Parliament and said so. It was agreed that he would address a political meeting in Oldham under Ascroft's sponsorship.

Before the meeting, however, Ascroft died suddenly. That left two seats vacant in Oldham, instead of one. The city is populated largely by workers in the cotton mills, and in order to capture this working class vote, the Conservative leadership in London hit upon a

novel plan. They would put up as their second candidate with Churchill a man who was known as a Socialist and who could claim to be a representative of the
cotton workers. Thus they would have, in Churchill,
a candidate of the aristocracy, and in the Socialist,
whose name was James Mawdsley, a member of the
working class. This would surely represent a ticket
which would appeal to all sections of the voters.

Unfortunately, it didn't. This being a by-election
(that is, one not regularly scheduled), it gave those who
were unhappy with the Conservative government a
chance of registering their discontent. The supporters
of the government, satisfied with their lot, did not go
to the polls. That was one factor. Another was that the
Conservatives had recently introduced a bill in the
House of Commons which would supply a livelihood
for Church of England clergymen. That was well
enough, but it brought opposition from other clergymen who were not members of the Church of England.

To give Churchill the credit due to him, he foresaw
this difficulty, and suggested that whatever money was
available should be divided up among clergymen of all
denominations according to the size of their flock. But
that idea pleased nobody and displeased everybody, so
he dropped it.

Churchill and Mawdsley made dozens of talks together to win the vote from their Liberal rivals, Alfred

Emmott, owner of a cotton factory, and Walter Runciman, wealthy son of the owner of a fleet of merchant ships. These two, whose personal fortunes far exceeded that of Churchill, denounced Winston as a representative of the privileged classes, and Mawdsley as a traitor to the working class.

Churchill enjoyed the campaign hugely, and got off a few barbs. Oldham being in Lancashire, he announced to the voters that "while the Lancashire Fusiliers were fighting for their country at Omdurman, Mr. Runciman was fighting for himself at Gravesend" (where the Runciman shipping interests had their headquarters). Praising the Conservative government, he pointed out that "never before were there so many people in England, and never before have they had so much to eat."

But when the votes were counted, Churchill and Mawdsley were defeated, and by a good margin.

This did not depress Winston. As has been noted before, he is always at his best in adversity.

When the election returns were announced, Churchill turned to Runciman and congratulated him on his victory. "I do not think the world has heard the last of either of us," he said, smiling cheerfully.

Like a great number of Churchill's prophecies, this one was to come true.

9

IN THE FALL of 1899, war broke out in South Africa between the British in Cape Colony and the Boers. The word "boer" comes from a Dutch word meaning "farmer." The Boers had formed a republic in the Transvaal, headed by President Paul Kruger. For some time, there had been growing enmity between the Boer Republic of the Transvaal and the British Cape Colony.

To protect their own people, the British sent troops to the borders of Transvaal. Kruger replied with an ultimatum saying that the troops were to be withdrawn in three days, and the war, to be known as the Boer War, was on.

It had hardly broken out before the *Morning Post* offered Churchill a thousand dollars a month, and all expenses, to cover it for them. This was the highest pay ever offered a British war correspondent up to that time, and Churchill accepted the job eagerly.

In London, it was thought that the war would be over in a matter of weeks. "How do you expect a group of untrained farmers to stand up to a British infantry division?" one high-placed officer asked Churchill. "The war will probably be over before you can get to South Africa. But I wish you luck."

Sir Redvers Buller was appointed British Commander in Chief and took the first ship, the "Dunottar Castle," to Capetown. Churchill, as correspondent of the *Morning Post,* went on the same ship. He wrote of the commander in chief later, "he was a man of a considerable scale. He plodded on from blunder to blunder and from one disaster to another, without losing either the regard of his country or the trust of his troops, to whose feeding as well as his own he paid serious attention."

The fact of the matter was that, after two generations of neglect, the British army was in no condition to fight a war. The Boers were all expert riflemen and riders. They had been arming steadily, receiving cannon, ammunition and rifles from Germany and Holland. But the British refused to pay any attention to this and expected the war to be over in three months at the most. Actually, it was three years before hostilities were brought to a close.

In those days there was no radio communication. The "Dunottar Castle" set out from England to South Africa, and for two weeks the Commander in Chief of the British forces was to be without any news whatever. He was not at all perturbed about this, feeling quite secure in his faith in the superiority of the British troops.

But when the ship arrived at Capetown, Sir Redvers learned that the Boers had successfully invaded the colony of Natal. That same day, in fact, though this was not known until later, the Boers had captured twelve hundred British troops and cut off the British force in Ladysmith.

The Boers had evolved a method of fighting against which the British were at a great disadvantage. They refused an open battle, but would appear suddenly and swiftly out of the wilderness to cut off groups of British soldiers. They called themselves commandos, and Churchill was much taken by their tactics. He was to use them later in World War II.

Meanwhile, Winston made immediate arrangements to get to the front in Natal and after a roundabout voyage, because it was impossible to go there direct, arrived at Estcourt where a small British force was in danger of being cut off by the Boers.

Forty miles to the north, and connected with Estcourt by a railroad, was Ladysmith, where a large British force was surrounded by the Boers. The British commander at Estcourt decided to send an armored train out towards Ladysmith to reconnoitre.

Churchill did not think the idea was very bright. However well armored a train might be, he pointed out, there was no way to protect the tracks on which it ran. The whole train could be sabotaged and destroyed, merely by pulling up a few rails. But the British commander laughed at the idea. A bunch of Dutch farmers would never have enough initiative to sabotage an armored train. That was his view. Besides, he would send a break-down gang with it. Captain J. A. Haldane, who was to command the train, told Churchill of the enterprise.

"I don't like it very much," he said, "though I'm keen to see some action. How would you like to come along with me?"

"I'd love to," said Churchill. "It'll provide a good story for the *Morning Post*."

A company of the Dublin Fusiliers and of the Durham Light Infantry was detailed to go with the train which also carried a six-pounder navy gun. The train was made up of six cars, the locomotive being placed in the center, so that it was pushing three and pulling three others. All went well for the first fourteen miles, and a stop was made at a small station to report the progress of the train by telegraph. But this was hardly done before a number of men were seen running toward the track.

"Boers," cried Churchill. "They're going to blow up the line."

"Turn back," Haldane ordered the engineer. The train started hurriedly for home. But it was too late. The Boers opened fire with two field guns. The train, gathering speed, rushed around a bend at about forty miles an hour, and suddenly there was a tremendous jar and everybody aboard was flung to the floor.

The Boers had sabotaged the line, as Churchill had feared, and the three cars ahead of the locomotive had been derailed.

Churchill and Haldane had a quick council of war. Obviously Haldane didn't think of Churchill as a civilian newspaperman, but as an officer of the army.

"If you'll defend us as best you can, I'll go forward and see whether the track can be cleared," Churchill suggested, and this was quickly agreed. The Boers were by now firing on the train with everything they had, including shrapnel shells. Churchill got to the engine to find the engineer bleeding from a face wound and highly indignant.

"Barbarians," he bellowed. "I'm a civilian. They're not supposed to fire on me. I quit right now. They might kill me. I won't have anything more to do with the train."

[77]

"Cheer up," said Churchill, "no man ever got wounded twice on the same day. I've been in the army a long time and I know. If you continue with your job, you're bound to get a medal for gallantry in the face of the enemy."

Under these persuasions, Churchill got the engineer back to work. But it was a long and dangerous job to clear the tracks so the locomotive could pull the three cars which were not derailed back to the safety of Estcourt. One of the cars had been thrown clear. But another was half on the tracks and half off it. This had to be butted off by the locomotive. All the while the Boers were firing and, with shrapnel bursting all around, the list of wounded mounted each minute.

The British had only rifles with which to reply. Shells from the Boer artillery flung into the sides of the armored train as Churchill worked, with nine volunteers, to clear the wreckage. Then came the job of hooking the locomotive to the three cars which had not been derailed. This, however, could not be done. The only thing to do was to load the wounded onto the locomotive and have the rest of the company retreat with the engine between them and the Boers.

But the soldiers could not keep up with the engine as it rolled down the track. Many of them fell behind, and Churchill leaped off the locomotive to rally them. He went back along the line on foot to where he believed Captain Haldane and the rest of the troops were.

But instead of finding them (they'd already been taken prisoner), he ran into two Boer commandos. Both fired at him and missed. Churchill scrambled up an embankment with bullets whistling around him, and found a small depression on the other side. Fifty yards away was a cabin in which he could find cover. He rose to sprint towards it. Suddenly a horseman dashed up and shouted a command to Churchill. The two men were only forty yards apart. Churchill reached for a revolver which he had been carrying, and then realized that he had left it on the train.

The horseman raised his rifle and called on Churchill to surrender. There was absolutely no chance to escape. Churchill shrugged his shoulders and raised his hands.

The man who had captured Churchill was Louis Botha, who later became a Boer general and later still the first Prime Minister of the Union of South Africa. Churchill and he became great friends in the years immediately before World War I, and Botha proved himself staunchly loyal to Britain during that struggle.

Meanwhile, Winston was Botha's prisoner. His capture was a great achievement for the Boers. It was not often that they took prisoner the son of an English lord. In vain Churchill stated that he was a war correspondent and, as a non-combatant, should be allowed to go free. The Boers knew well that he was responsible for the escape of the locomotive with the wounded English soldiers aboard. They decided that he would be sent to their capital, Pretoria, and imprisoned there.

But they did not know their man, and as soon as Churchill arrived in the prison camp in Pretoria, he started planning to escape.

Winston found Captain Haldane at the camp, and the two put their heads together. Churchill thought up some of the fanciest schemes for escaping from a prison outside the pages of romance. One involved not only escape but the capture of the city of Pretoria. Haldane expressed his admiration of all these plans, but sensibly pointed out that they wouldn't work.

"You've got to be simple about these things, Winnie," he said. "The simpler the better."

"How about just climbing over the stockade at dawn tomorrow and just walking off?" Churchill said.

"Good, if you can find a place that isn't guarded," was Haldane's reply.

Churchill did find a portion of the stockade which was not in view of the sentries posted around. Then he went boldly to the prison commissary and bought a suit of civilian clothing. He bought a good suit, paying twenty pounds (about eighty dollars) for it, and

the commissary officials asumed that the son of an English lord wanted to be smartly dressed even in a prison
camp. But Churchill had other ideas.

In the same prison camp with him was a Boer clergyman, confined for some petty offense. Churchill,
though of a devout nature, stole the clergyman's hat,
deciding it would be useful.

Inside the prison compound there were two lava-
tories, housed in circular buildings. These stood near
the wall of the compound, and cut the top of the wall
off from view of the sentry. Churchill decided it would
be simple to climb to the top of the lavatory from inside, get onto the "blind spot" on the wall, and make
his escape. Two other officers were to join him in the
attempt, his friend Captain Haldane and a Lieutenant
Brockie.

Churchill went first. He waited until the sentry had
walked away and stopped for a chat with a fellow
guard. Then Churchill climbed to the lavatory roof.
There was one bad moment when his waistcoat caught
on the ornamental masonry at the top. He was in full
view of both sentries but managed to free himself without attracting their attention. Then he dropped over
the side of the prison wall to find himself in a private
garden. He waited, crouched in some bushes, for his
companions to join him.

They didn't come.

Churchill decided to signal them and coughed loudly. Suddenly one of the conspirators started talking a lot of nonsense and laughing wildly. The other said above the babble, "It's all up. The sentries are suspicious. Can you get back in?"

Get back in after going to all the trouble of climbing out? Churchill had no intention of doing any such thing. One of the officers who was to have escaped with him, and had now been prevented from doing so, could talk Dutch. Churchill knew not a word of the language. He was three hundred miles from the nearest neutral territory, Delagoa Bay in Portuguese East Africa, he had only four bars of chocolate as a source of nourishment, and had no map or compass. Still, he believed he would be able to give the Boers a good run for their money before he was recaptured. Certainly he was not going to return to prison voluntarily. So he pulled his clergyman's hat down over his eyes, stepped out of the garden into the road, and went on his way humming a little tune to himself.

Churchill's luck has rarely run out on him for long. In the midst of the Boer capital, without the ability to inquire his way, and with no knowledge of the city, he decided he must find a railroad and steal a ride on a train. He had no idea where a railroad was to be found, nor whether any train he caught would take him to Delagoa Bay or deeper into Boer Territory. He decided to follow the road on which he found himself. The road led through the middle of the town. Churchill walked along the center of the street, tipping his hat to various townspeople as he passed by. When he reached the outskirts of the city, he found a railroad line.

The track did not seem to lead to Portuguese territory however. It was headed north and Delagoa Bay was to the east. Still, Churchill decided that he would board the first train that passed by and trust to luck that it would take him in the right direction.

Once more his luck held. He caught the train, leaping onto a car half full of empty coal sacks. After a little while, the train changed its direction from north to east. This Churchill knew by studying the stars. The train was going in the right direction, and he fell asleep.

Winston was awake before dawn, conscious of the fact that his escape must now be known and trains would be searched for him. He must then leave the train and hide during the day. The whole countryside had indeed been roused and a reward of twenty-five pounds had been offered for him, dead or alive. Churchill later complained that this was a small sum, and he was surely worth more than that, particularly alive.

When he left the train he found a grove of trees and

hid in this during the hot South African day which
followed. He had for his companion a large vulture
which kept examining him with speculative eyes. Winston wished he had more than the four bars of chocolate (one of which he had already eaten) to keep him
alive.

During the day he suffered very much from thirst
but dared not leave the shelter of the trees to drink at
a small pond half a mile away. When night came again,
he drank his fill and then waited for a train to pass
along the track.

Hour after hour passed by and still no train came.
By one in the morning he had decided that a new
order had been issued and no more trains were running at night. That meant he must walk to the Portuguese border, which he now believed to be about two
hundred and thirty miles distant.

He set out. But soon the hopelessness of the task
became apparent to him. Off to the side he could see
some lights, perhaps from a farmhouse. He had money
in his pocket. Perhaps he could bribe the people in
the farmhouse to assist him—give him a guide and a
pony. At least it was worth trying.

Again Churchill's luck was with him. The lights did
not come from a farmhouse but from the works around
the top of a coal mine. The coal mine was in charge of
two Scotsmen and two Englishmen, whom the Boers

had allowed to stay to keep the mine in working condition until the war was over. The coal mine was in fact the only place within twenty miles that Churchill could have gone for help without immediately being handed over to the Boers.

The manager of the mine, John Howard, immediately gave Winston food and shelter and, with the other three, agreed to hide him in the bottom of the pit until the hue and cry had died down. One of the miners was from Oldham, Lancashire, where Churchill had been an unsuccessful candidate for Parliament.

"They'll all vote for you next time, Mr. Churchill," he said, giving him a hearty handshake.

Churchill remained several days in the mine while plans were made to evacuate him by train to Portuguese territory. To do this, the aid of a Boer who was a British sympathizer had to be obtained. This man's name was Burgener, and he had a load of cotton bales to send to Lourenco Marques in Portuguese Delagoa Bay. Churchill was smuggled into one of the railroad cars carrying the bales, with plenty of food and a pistol. He reached Lourenco Marques without further mishap. When the train carrying him crossed into Portuguese Territory, Winston could not resist pulling out his revolver and firing three or four triumphant shots into the air.

From Lourenco Marques, Churchill, with the aid of

the British Consul, took the steamer to Durban and arrived to find himself a national hero. For days every kind of story about him had been printed in the British papers. Some reports said he had been shot; others that he had been captured; others that he was being hidden by British sympathizers in Pretoria.

The British had suffered heavy military reverses in the Boer War up to that time. Churchill's escape was the one bright item of news there had been in weeks. Those who had escaped with the armored train attributed their freedom to him. Several correspondents stated that he should have been given the Victoria Cross for saving the armored train.

Churchill was a national hero. But the war was still raging and he decided that he ought to do more than report it. He ought, as a patriotic Briton, to join the army again.

10

Winston Churchill might be able to claim a record for fighting in wars without being paid for his services. At the Battle of Omdurman he was an unpaid officer, and he was given a commision in the South African Light Horse by Sir Redvers Buller, the Commander in Chief, on condition that he receive no salary. What money he earned would be as a war correspondent for the *Morning Post*.

But the Boer War was to prove enormously important to Churchill in later years. During its course, he saw at first hand, in the operations of the Boer commandos, how civilians well-acquainted with the country in which they were fighting, and well-trained in the use of a rifle, could fight professional soldiers to a standstill. From that demonstration came the commandos which he originated as troops in World War II. He also saw how unimaginative generals, slow to move, often lost priceless advantages and, quite as often, blundered into traps laid for them by the enemy.

Churchill not only saw these things firsthand, but had the courage to report them to his newspaper. This made him unpopular in England for a while. One Boer, he wrote, was the equivalent of three to five regular professional soldiers. The answer was to train the regular soldiers of the British Army up to the standards of intelligence and character of the Boer fighters, or use five times as many British soldiers as Boers. There was a loud outcry against Winston when he reported this. But not many months later, his advice was taken, and so many British troops poured into the Boer War that the Boers had no chance against them.

Again Churchill pleaded for lenience toward the Boers when they were defeated. This also made him unpopular in many quarters, particularly in the British areas of South Africa. But Churchill stuck to his guns, as he always did.

While he was creating all this furore by his reports in the *Morning Post,* Churchill was having fun on the battlefields of South Africa. As an unpaid officer but a salaried newspaperman, he was able to move about freely from one unit to another. So he could get into any kind of action that was going on.

On one occasion, in a cavalry skirmish at Dewetsdorp, the girth holding the saddle on his horse was

Winston Churchill as a small boy, the determination of his nature already plainly showing in his face.

Blenheim Palace, where Churchill was born on November 30th, 1874, son of an American mother and an English lord.

Harrow, the public school where Churchill's formal education began.

Young Winston in the rather elaborate dress worn by small boys of his day.

Lt. Winston Churchill
wearing the uniform
the 4th Hussars.

Sandhurst, the British equivalent of West Point. It was at Sandhurst that Churchill began his military training.

t twenty-six Churchill as elected to a Conservive seat in Parliament.

Churchill in 1899 in the uniform of the South African Light Horse.

Right: Now famous, after his fabulous escape from the Boer prison, Churchill boards a ship in Durban to return to England and start a political career.

An artist's impression of a battle scene in the Boer War.

Churchill as First Lord of the Admiralty with his great friend and admirer Earl Lloyd George.

Churchill about to take a flight in one of the first airplanes ever built.

Churchill in 1919 at which time he was Secretary for the British Colonies.

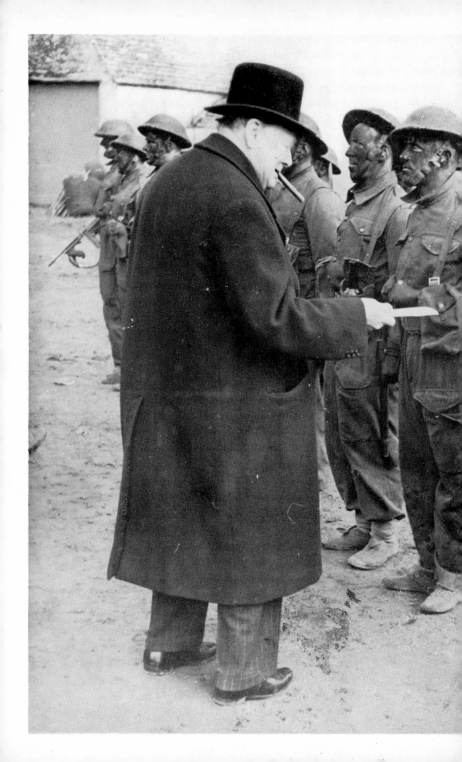

The Prime Minister inspects the knife of a Commando. He was first impressed by guerilla warfare during the Boer War, when he saw how effective it was against a well-trained British army; however, he was not able to form a British Commando force until 1942 when this picture was taken.

Honorary Air Commodore of the Royal Auxiliary Airforce, the Prime Minister gives his famous salute to the people of England, a V for victory.

shot through and Churchill was thrown to the ground. He got up to find himself a running target for four or five Boers. He could see himself either killed or back in the Boer prison in Pretoria, when a British trooper came flying by.

"Lend me a stirrup," Churchill shouted.

"Jump up behind," yelled the trooper, reining in his horse.

Churchill leapt up behind the man in a second and the two were off. The trooper kept swearing because the Boers had wounded his horse.

"Never mind the horse," said Churchill. "You've saved my life."

"It's the horse I'm worried about," said the trooper, more concerned with his mount than with the future Prime Minister of Britain. The man was later awarded the Distinguished Conduct Medal for saving Churchill.

On another occasion, two British armies were lying one on each side of Johannesburg. The city was in the hands of the Boers, and the two generals had no quick means of communicating with each other. Yet urgent messages had to be passed between them. Churchill noticed that quite a few civilians were going in and out of the city and the Boers didn't stop them or interfere with them. So he borrowed a bicycle and some civilian clothes and volunteered to ride through the city, which was in enemy hands, with messages for the British general on the other side.

He found Johannesburg thick with Boers. But there was only one bad moment. That came when a mounted Boer policeman pulled his horse to walk beside Churchill and looked at him hard for a long time. Churchill just stared back and, after a while, the policeman went on his way.

For some months, as already stated, a British army had been besieged in Ladysmith by the Boers. Churchill scooped all the other British war correspondents by requisitioning a horse and being the first British horseman to ride into the city when the siege was lifted. He was even ahead of the British cavalry.

He, with his cousin, the eighth Duke of Marlborough, were also the first to enter Pretoria when the Boer city, in which Churchill had been a prisoner, surrendered. The two of them persuaded eighty-five prison guards at the prisoner of war camp in which British officers and soldiers were held to surrender to them. Some of the men in prison had been there when Churchill made his remarkable escape. They said they were quite sure that he would be back to liberate them.

During all his time in the Boer War, Churchill was never wounded. His younger brother, John (or Jack as he was called in the family), was wounded in the leg, however, in a skirmish during his first few hours at the front. John Churchill later became one of Britain's most capable soldiers although, since he did not enter political life, he was scarcely known at all. He was a major in World War I and was mentioned in dispatches for bravery and given the Distinguished Service Order. But when he died in 1947 it came as a surprise to many people in both Britain and the United States to learn that Winston Churchill had a brother.

Winston Churchill had one final adventure before he left South Africa. The war was not over. Most of the larger cities had been captured by the British. But many months of guerilla warfare still lay ahead. However, Churchill knew that a general election was certain to be held soon and he wanted to be a candidate for a seat in Parliament. So he resigned his commission in the army and his position as war correspondent on the *Morning Post.*

On the way to Cape Town, where he would catch a ship to England, the train on which he was traveling was shelled by the Boers. The train was full of soldiers who jumped out, but there were no officers to give them orders. Churchill assumed command. The incident reminded him too much of the time he had been shelled in the armored train, and made a prisoner of war, not to interfere. Churchill ran to the engineer's cab and ordered the engineer to give three or four blasts on his whistle as a signal to the soldiers to get back aboard.

Then he told the engineer to back up to the last station they had left, which Churchill knew was fortified. It was wise that he did so. A bridge ahead had been burned, and a train which had gone through only a little while previously was attacked by the Boers who killed or wounded sixty of those aboard.

So Winston Churchill's adventures in South Africa during the Boer War started and ended with an attack upon a train in which he was traveling.

11

THE BRITISH general election of 1900, in which Winston Churchill was to make his second bid to enter Parliament, became known as the "khaki election." With the Boer War still in progress, it was plain that the issues of the campaign would center around the war. Had it been necessary? Or could an understanding have been reached with the Boers without a war? Was the war being efficiently conducted? What should be the terms of settlement when the fighting ceased? These were the questions uppermost in the minds of the voters who were shortly to go to the polls and elect a new Parliament.

Churchill's party, the Conservatives, led by Lord Salisbury, maintained that the war was necessary and had been forced on the British. The Liberals said that more tolerance and appreciation of the position of the Dutch in South Africa would have avoided the conflict.

The Conservatives held that the war must be fought until every last Boer had laid down his arms. "Unconditional surrender" was their war policy. The Liberals felt that negotiations for peace should be started without unconditional surrender. An armistice should be arranged and the peace terms discussed without the Boers being utterly defeated.

Churchill flung himself into the political arena with the greatest zest. He practiced the speeches he would make in the campaign on the voyage from South Africa to England, addressing himself to the waves of the ocean and any passengers aboard who would listen to him.

He knew exactly where he stood. The war had been unavoidable because the aggression had come from the Boers. It had to be fought to complete victory. But thereafter the hand of friendship must be extended to the Boers and the wounds of war healed as quickly as possible.

He decided to stand for election in Oldham, where he had been defeated in his first try to enter Parliament. But now he had many factors on his side. He was a veteran of the Boer War and had observed the fighting at first hand. His reports to the *Morning Post* had made him famous and an authority on the issues involved. He had made a brilliant escape from the

Boers. And his escape had been aided by the miner from Oldham, whose name was Dewsnap.

Oldham received Churchill with open arms and rowdy demonstrations of enthusiasm. He gave a great deal of credit for his escape to the Oldham man who had aided him. He was a winning candidate from the day he arrived in the city to start his campaign. People turned out in thousands to hear him.

Two seats were to be contested in the election. When the votes were counted, after Churchill had addressed one hundred and fifty meetings in two months, he was elected by a comfortable majority.

In those days the whole nation did not vote on one day. The elections were spread out over a period of six weeks. Oldham voted among the first and, when Churchill was elected, it became his duty to help other Conservative candidates to win.

So for the next six weeks Churchill toured Britain, appearing on one platform after another in support of Conservative candidates. He met all the great Conservative leaders of his time—Lord Salisbury, the head of the party, Joseph Chamberlain, the colonial secretary, and Arthur Balfour who was to become First Lord of the Treasury. Quite often his appearance on the platform roused greater enthusiasm than that of the more famous men he had come to help. He was riding the crest of an enormous wave of popularity, and was one of the most famous figures in England. When the election was over, the Conservatives had obtained a large majority.

Churchill now turned to the matter of his personal finances. He was twenty-five years of age, a member of Parliament, had published five books, was a professional soldier who had seen more active service than many officers of much higher rank, and a well-known journalist. Members of the British Parliament in those days received no salary. After resigning from the army, Winston had no income, and though his books were selling well, they did not bring in enough to assure him full financial independence.

Churchill, therefore, decided to spend a few months as a lecturer. He would make a tour of Britain and then go to the United States. The proceeds should be sufficient to keep him for some years.

His English lectures, in which he talked of the Boer War and his other adventures, were an overwhelming success. People lined up for hours to get into the hall in which he was to talk. The most famous men of England were glad to introduce him as the speaker. Lord Wolseley launched him on his lecture tour in St. James's Hall, London. Sir Arthur Conan Doyle, the inventor of Sherlock Holmes, was chairman at his second lecture. Lord Rosebery introduced him at Edinburgh. His average was five hundred dollars a night during his English tour, and when it ended he had saved about twenty thousand dollars.

Then he tackled America, and met a very different reaction. In England, Churchill was a hero and the Boer War, on the whole, was popular. In America, Churchill was not a hero. He was an Englishman, coming from a privileged class. And Americans of Irish descent were hostile to him. Furthermore many Americans sympathized with the Boers. So Churchill mounted his first lecture platform in New York to face an audience which was decidedly cool. They heard him through but gave him no great ovation. The audience was not very large and quite a number had come to see Samuel L. Clemens who, under the name Mark Twain, had achieved lasting fame as a humorist and writer. In introducing Churchill to his first American audience, Mark Twain said something about him of which Churchill has been proud ever since. Twain said, "Ladies and gentlemen, the lecturer tonight is Mr. Winston Churchill. By his father he is an Englishman, by his mother an American. Behold the perfect man."

In Chicago, a city with a heavy Irish population, Churchill faced his most hostile American audience. A large number of Irish-Americans were present when he started his lecture, and they interrupted him frequently with boos and hisses. Whenever he mentioned

[97]

the British they booed, and whenever he mentioned the Boers they cheered.

But Churchill by now had found the remedy. He was describing a situation in which the British Army was being hard pressed by the Boers and the Irishmen were cheering for the Boers and hissing at the British, producing enormous confusion.

Churchill raised his voice above the hubbub and roared, "Then the Dublin Fusiliers were called forward. The trumpets sounded the charge, and the enemy were swept from the field." The Irish-American audience roared with delight and paid Churchill respectful and sympathetic attention from that moment. Thereafter, when facing an American audience made up largely of Irish immigrants or descendants of Irish immigrants, Churchill always called upon the Dublin Fusiliers to help. Without a doubt, the Fusiliers made more charges on the lecture platform than on the bloodied battlefields of South Africa. But such scruples did not deter Churchill who learned in the United States a good lesson in dealing with unfriendly audiences.

By the time he returned to England, to take his seat in Parliament, Winston Churchill had received from his lectures forty thousand dollars. He was ready to start his unpaid career as a politician with adequate financial reserves which he had earned himself.

Few men have entered Parliament with such prospects of a great future as Winston Churchill. Brilliant as he was himself, he was also the son of a brilliant father. Lord Randolph Churchill had been one of the greatest orators in the House of Commons in his day. His thinking had been daring and in many respects in advance of his times. He had wanted more advantages for the working men of England. He had wanted a more generous policy toward the people of India. Frequently his ideas brought him in conflict with the Conservative Party to which he belonged. When such conflicts arose, he always threatened to resign, and he usually won his case. As we have seen, however, he resigned once too often, and that resignation ended his political career.

It was expected of Winston Churchill, then, that he would also be a brilliant orator and a daring thinker. But it was hoped that, unlike his father, he would put loyalty to the party before his personal beliefs.

Churchill started his political career with a warning of storms to come. In the House of Commons great importance is rightly attached to eloquence. The first speech of a new member of Parliament is a very important event in his political life. Churchill received notice that he would be given the floor for his first speech during a debate on the Boer War. A member of the opposition party, the Liberals, who had a reputation for eloquence and whose name was David Lloyd George, would move a minor amendment to the government resolution on the Boer War.

When he had moved his amendment, Churchill would be allowed to make his maiden speech in reply to it. Churchill worked on his speech for a month. In those days he liked to write his speeches out and, relying on the phenomenal memory which had made him the master of the *Lays of Ancient Rome* while he was at Harrow, recite them at the appropriate time.

Thus, he had his speech memorized when David Lloyd George arose to move his amendment. But to Churchill's horror, when Lloyd George arose, he announced that he would not move any amendment, but would speak instead on the general subject of the Boer War.

Churchill realized that his whole speech based upon Lloyd George's amendment was out the window, unless he could devise some method of introducing it with a happy phrase. As David Lloyd George rolled on (and he had all the eloquence of the Welsh), Churchill listened with all his powers of concentration, trying to find some phrase to which he could hook his prepared speech. But none was offered. The time when he would have to talk himself drew closer and closer and still he had not found a single note with which to introduce his prepared address.

Lloyd George's address was stormy and violent. Churchill was in despair. Then a member, sitting close to him, and sensing his predicament, leaned over and whispered, "You might say: instead of making his violent speech without moving his moderate amendment, he had better have moved his moderate amendment without making his violent speech."

That was just the phrase that Churchill had been searching for desperately. When Lloyd George sat down, Winston was ready with his opening sentence.

It was received with a cheer. But a few sentences later the Conservative Party groaned.

It was part of the party's platform that the Boers were in the wrong, and deserving of no sympathy or consideration. Churchill admired the Boers as magnificent fighters. He would not allow loyalty to the Conservative Party line to interfere with his admiration for the enemy. So he said, ". . . the Boers who are fighting in the field—and if I were a Boer, I hope I should be fighting in the field . . ." There were gasps of dismay from the Conservative benches around him. Conservative members whispered, "Just like his father. Rebellious." The opposition Liberals cheered.

Churchill, in his very first speech, had served notice to the House of Commons that, party or no party, he would speak his mind and do as he thought right, just like his father, Lord Randolph.

12

I T WAS QUITE OBVIOUS, from the time of his first speech in Parliament, that Winston Churchill and the Conservative Party would part company sooner or later. The Conservatives insisted upon the harshest treatment of the Boers. Churchill insisted equally that the Boers should be treated with respect and humanity. The issue was as simple as that to start with.

However, other issues arose, and Churchill found he could not accept them quietly, out of loyalty to the party. He had to state his views which agreed more and more with those of the Liberals. His fellow Conservatives grew increasingly angry with him.

The issue of the army estimates arose. The Boer War had shown that the British army was sadly lacking both in men and modern equipment. More money was needed to supply both. Churchill's wider vision made it clear to him that Britain, being an island, should rely more heavily on its navy than its army. With a powerful navy the country could fight its battles "at arm's length," in other words on the oceans and seas of the world. This was not the view of the Conservative Party. But it was Churchill's view and he intended to express it.

"Has the English Channel dried up, and are we no longer an island?" he demanded in the House of Commons, while his fellow Conservatives shook their heads and looked wrathfully at him.

"The honor and security of the British Empire do not depend, and can never depend, upon the British army," he continued. "The Admiralty is the only office strong enough to insure the British Empire."

This had been his father's stand, and Churchill, who was at the time engaged in writing a two-volume biography of his father, was well aware of it.

Soon Churchill became so unpopular with his fellow Conservatives that one day, when he arose to address the House of Commons, they all got up and walked out. Churchill blanched and went on with his address. His time, he knew, would come.

The depth of the gap between Winston and the Conservatives increased daily. Churchill would do nothing to heal it. On the contrary, being in his favorite position—that is, outnumbered and with the odds against him—he revelled in the battle.

He was not quite alone. A few of the younger Conservatives agreed with him, among them Ian Malcolm, Lord Hugh Cecil, and Ivor Guest, who later became Lord Wimborne. They were called "The Malcolmtents" by the press, which took relish in the situation.

A revered figure in the Conservative Party was Joseph Chamberlain, Chancellor of the Exchequer. The Conservatives, seeking more sources of revenue, had come out in favor of tariffs. That is, they wished to make people exporting goods to England from other countries pay duty on those goods. The duties paid went to the British treasury. Chamberlain was one of the leading supporters of tariffs. Churchill entirely disagreed with the idea. He maintained that tariffs would make food and clothing dearer for the working men of Britain.

When Chamberlain set out on a speaking tour of the country, preaching tariffs, Churchill and Cecil, who was his cousin, followed behind, speaking against tariffs. This was political impertinence of a high degree. But Churchill planned more, for he now completely disagreed with the Conservatives. He wrote to one Liberal candidate seeking election and wished him well—the equivalent of a Democrat in the United States wishing a Republican candidate for the Congress victory over his Democratic rival.

At a political meeting in Halifax, he ended a speech

with the cry, "Thank God we have a Liberal Party."

Once, when a Liberal member was speaking in the House, Churchill arose to make a complaint to the Speaker (or chairman) of the House. "Mr. Speaker," he said, "I rise to a point of order. I am quite unable to hear what my honorable friend is saying owing to the vulgar clamor maintained by the Conservative Party."

The Conservatives against whom he was in rebellion fought back with all the eloquence at their disposal. But they were handicapped, having mastered Latin and Greek at school, while Churchill was mastering English.

A certain Colonel Kenyon-Slaney, in an unguarded moment, called Churchill a traitor.

"I have noticed," Churchill cried, "that when political controversy becomes excited, persons of choleric dispositions and limited intelligence are apt to be rude. If I was a traitor, at any rate I was fighting the Boers in South Africa when Colonel Kenyon-Slaney was slandering them at home. . . ."

Churchill's time came when a young Conservative arose to inform the House that he had heard there was an outbreak of the disease beri-beri in South Africa. An unmistakable symptom of the disease, he said, was a distinct swelling of the head. The inference that Churchill, long in South Africa, was suffering from a swelled head, brought roars of laughter from the Conservative benches.

The House of Commons is traditionally divided into two sides. The government party sits on one side; Her Majesty's Loyal Opposition on the other. Down the middle runs a bench for members to put their notes, briefcases, and hats upon. To cross from one side of the House to the other serves official and public notice of changing party.

After the beri-beri incident, Churchill picked up his silk hat, looked around at the grinning Conservatives and, amidst rousing cheers from the Liberals, crossed over the floor of the House, and sat down on the Liberal benches beside Lloyd George.

Winston Churchill, only four years in Parliament, and thus very much of a junior member, had turned his back on all the influential men in the Conservative Party, to join the opposition. Next time he stood for election it would be as a candidate of the minority party, and he would have a hard fight. Yet he was not prepared to sacrifice his principles merely to retain influential Conservative friends and keep a safe seat in Parliament.

By this time Churchill had already won an enviable reputation for himself as an orator in the House of Commons; and not only an orator but something of a prophet too.

In 1901, looking toward the great wars of the future, then unsuspected, he warned the House, "The wars of peoples will be more terrible than those of kings."

Once an opposition member was so wrathful over something Churchill was saying that he made rumbling noises of indignation. Churchill silenced him with the words, "My right honorable friend should not develop more indignation than he can contain."

Not much later in his career there was some sniping at him in Parliament over his writing. It was said that he was making a profit out of his public life. Churchill turned to his fellow members and said, "Leave the past to History, particularly since I intend to write it myself." That silenced the critics.

When Joseph Chamberlain, Chancellor of the Exchequer, was pressing for tariffs to which, as stated, Churchill was opposed, Churchill arose to say, "Mr. Chamberlain loves the working man. He loves to see him work."

To quit the Conservative Party and throw in his lot with the Liberals required a great deal of moral courage. As it turned out, the move was the very best that Churchill could have made in every way.

The Conservatives, long in power, had lost their grip upon the country. They had managed to prolong their life by calling an election at the peak of success in the Boer War—the "khaki election" spoken of

earlier. But the party had lost touch with the real de-
sires of the voters. Under the British constitution, the
majority party, if defeated on a major issue in the
House of Commons, asks for a vote of confidence from
the House. If the House votes no confidence in the government, it is the duty of the Prime Minister to tender
his resignation to the sovereign.

That is what happened to the Conservative Party
shortly after Churchill had crossed over to the Liberals.
Mr. Arthur Balfour, the Conservative Prime Minister
was compelled to resign, and King Edward VII who
had succeeded Queen Victoria on the throne, asked the
leader of the Liberals, Sir Henry Campbell-Bannerman, to form a government.

Sir Henry made a bold decision in making up his
cabinet. He appointed Churchill Under Secretary of
State for the Colonies. Thus, at the age of thirty-one,
and after only five years in Parliament, Winston
Churchill became a British Cabinet minister.

13

CHURCHILL'S FIRST cabinet post, Under Secretary for the Colonies, did not last long. He received the appointment in 1905 and in 1906 a general election was to be held in Britain. Now Churchill no longer had the support of influential and wealthy men in securing a seat in the new Parliament. Indeed the Marlborough family refused to have anything to do with him, feeling that in joining the Liberals, Winston had deserted the traditional party of his father and grandfather, the Duke of Marlborough.

But the Liberals, with many brilliant men in the lead, including David Lloyd George, John Morley, and Sir Edward Grey, rallied to his support.

The election campaign was one of the most exciting and hard-fought in the present century. The principal issue was tariffs versus free trade. Churchill's mother, Lady Randolph, entered the fray by the side of her son.

It is said that she told the voters to make their choice between "dear food and dear Winston." In the forefront of the election was the vigorous and at times rowdy demand of the women of England to be allowed to vote. Demanding suffrage, that is, the right to vote, they became known as suffragettes and were led by Sylvia Pankhurst.

Unfortunately for Churchill, the suffragettes picked him as a target of attack. Just why they did so is hard to discover. Perhaps it was because he represented the essence of masculinity in a land ruled, at that time, by men.

Winston's relationship with women up to that time had always been courteous but distant. He was not above rebuking women who disagreed with him. On one occasion, a lady at a dinner party, no doubt offended by Churchill monopolizing the conversation (which he often did), said to him, "Mr. Churchill, I like neither your politics nor your mustache." To this Churchill replied, "Do not distress yourself, madam. You are not likely to come into close contact with either of them."

Churchill was to contest a seat in northwest Manchester. The suffragettes swarmed to his meetings. They pelted his election posters with apricots, and at one meeting formed a flying wedge and swept through the audience, knocking people off their feet. Many people were hurt in the riot that followed and Miss Pankhurst and her chief lieutenant, a Miss Kenney, went to jail for disturbing the peace. Churchill gallantly offered to bail both out, but was met with the reply that the ladies refused to be bailed out by anyone in pants.

When the two were released, and with the campaign in full swing, pictures of Miss Pankhurst and Miss Kenney were plastered over all the Churchill election posters. Churchill, who had fought dervishes in the Sudan, Pathans in Afghanistan, and Boers in South Africa, found himself facing a foe with whom he had no experience and against whom it was impossible to fight with anything but words.

He tried compromise and invited Miss Pankhurst up to his election platform to ask questions.

She, however, kept saying, "Yah! Yah! Yah!" every time she had put a question, making it quite impossible for Churchill to reply. Finally he made a firm stand over the slightly hysterical interruptions of the suffragette leader.

"Nothing will induce me to vote for giving women the franchise," he said. "I will not be henpecked into a question of such importance."

Long after the election Churchill was horsewhipped by a suffragette who believed he had said that *they* ought to be horsewhipped, which was untrue. The suffragette in question struck him across the face with a whip as he was getting down from a train. Churchill said he would not dream of taking the assault personally and refused to proceed against her.

It is possible that Churchill was really in sympathy with the suffragettes and admired their courage though not their tactics. Perhaps if they had taken another approach he would have been on their side. But he would never support them (or anyone else) under pressure, and so became their opponent.

Once some suffragettes had chained themselves to the railings around the Houses of Parliament declaring that they would never loose their chains until they had been given the vote. To this Churchill said, "A man might as well chain himself to the railings of St. Thomas' Hospital declaring that he would remain there until he had a baby." The quip angered the suffragettes even further.

Churchill's opponent in the critical election of 1906 was a London lawyer named Joynson-Hicks. He had none of Churchill's dash or popularity, and in spite of the troubles with the suffragettes, when the votes were counted, Churchill had won.

His victory was the more significant because Arthur Balfour, leader of the Conservative Party, who was contesting a seat in northeast Manchester, was defeated. Churchill rose as the old guard Conservatives fell, and when the final results were in, the Liberals held the majority by a good margin in the House of Commons.

Churchill was naturally appointed once more to the cabinet post of Under Secretary for the Colonies. The Secretary for the Colonies, his chief, was a member of the Upper House of the British Parliament, the House of Lords. He was content to leave a great deal of the work in Churchill's hands, and Winston threw all his untiring energy into his work.

The post was no mere empty title. The whole of the South African problem came under the Colonial Office, and so Churchill, who had fought in the Boer War, had come to respect the Boers, had pleaded for generous treatment of them, now had the power to ensure that generous treatment was accorded to them. Churchill had a large hand in bringing about the eventual establishment of the Union of South Africa.

On the Boer side in these negotiations, he dealt with the man who had captured him during the battle of the armored train, General Botha, who became the first Prime Minister of the Union of South Africa. Churchill and Botha, enemies on the battlefield, were fast friends in peace. The friendship proved of especial value during World War I, when Botha rallied South Africa to the support of his former foes, the British, against the Germans.

Winston Churchill's career has never been serene.

He once said of himself, "I have a tendency against which I should, perhaps, be on my guard, to swim against the stream."

And even when he wanted to swim with the stream, sometimes the stream turned unexpectedly and went against him.

Such an unexpected about-face occurred shortly after winning the election to Parliament as the Liberal member for northwest Manchester. In 1908, Campbell-Bannerman, leader of the Liberals and Prime Minister, resigned as a result of illness. His place was taken by Mr. Henry Asquith, and in the cabinet changes that followed, Churchill had the misfortune to be appointed President of the Board of Trade.

The post was a promotion from that of Under Secretary for the Colonies. But it was peculiar in that anyone appointed President of the Board of Trade had to seek re-election to Parliament.

Churchill had to go back to the voters again, and this time matters went badly for him. The suffragettes entered violently into the campaign against him. Mobs of them turned out at all his political rallies to shout him down and create a riot. His opponent was once more Joynson-Hicks, and when the votes were counted, Churchill was out and Joynson-Hicks was in. A cabinet promotion had cost Winston Churchill his seat in

Parliament in the fickle and stormy political atmosphere of the day!

But there was a silver lining.

As Churchill left the Manchester Reform Club after learning of his defeat, he was handed a telegram. It contained a request that he stand for election in Dundee where a vacancy had occurred.

Off Winston went, and though again harassed by a suffragette who rang a handbell through all his meetings, Churchill was victorious. Another and perhaps greater success lay ahead of him.

Though thirty-three years of age, Winston Churchill in 1908 had shown very little interest in women. There were no romances in his career up to that time. But now he had fallen in love with a Miss Clementine Hozier, daughter of Sir H. M. Hozier. Her mother was Lady Blanche Ogilvy and the family was one of the most notable in Dundee. Indeed, it was through them that Churchill was offered the chance to contest the Dundee election.

He and Miss Hozier were married in St. Margaret's Church, Westminster, London. All the bluebloods of England and all the notables of the political world turned out for the ceremony. The couple's wedding presents included gifts from the King and Queen and every member of the Cabinet.

Some said that Churchill was so unpredictable and

individualistic that the marriage would not last six months. Churchill, writing of it later, said that from the day of his wedding he lived happily ever after. He had five children, a son Randolph, who followed him into politics, and four daughters, Diana, Sarah, Mary, and Margaret Frances. The latter died as a young girl. Diana, Sarah, and Mary are now all married.

England at the turn of the twentieth century was a land sharply divided into classes. In the great industrial towns of Birmingham, London, Manchester, and Liverpool, poverty and squalor abounded among the working people. This contrasted sharply with the lavish lives lived by the nobility and the wealthy manufacturers who sat down to six and seven course dinners at which several kinds of wine were served. On the one hand was grim poverty and on the other lavish expenditure.

Winston Churchill was a stranger to poverty. In contrast to the toiling millions in the factories, many of whom were undernourished children and women, Churchill had never had to wonder where his next meal was coming from.

He came to realize that poverty existed in England, and on a large scale, during his election campaigns in Manchester and Dundee. The death of Mrs. Everest, his old nurse, many years before, had awakened him to the fact that thousands of people, when their working life was done, had nothing to support them in their old age other than the charity of their relatives.

He now threw himself into the battle to provide better living conditions for what he called "the submerged tenth" of English men and women. From the Board of Trade he was quickly appointed to the Home Office. He pushed through Parliament an act guaranteeing a minimum wage in industries notorious for sweated labor, threw all the force of his mind and eloquence behind laws to establish old age pensions, to limit working hours in mines to eight per day, to regulate the employment of children in factories and to set up labor exchanges (employment bureaus) where those out of work could find jobs.

Churchill was not a Socialist and has always disliked Socialism. But he was accused of being a Socialist when he sought these reforms, and he replied deftly.

"I look forward to the universal establishment of minimum standards of life and labor, and their progressive elevation as the increasing energies of production may permit," he told a Glasgow meeting. "I do not think that liberalism in any circumstances can cut itself off from this fertile field of social effort, and I would recommend you not to be scared in discussing any of these proposals, just because some old woman comes along and tells you they are socialistic."

Of Communism he said early in his career that it was

a ghoul descending from a pile of skulls. Nothing in his later life changed that basic view.

Communism was already beginning to make an appearance in the slums of London at this time. As Home Secretary, Churchill was responsible for the police. This brought him early into the fight against Communism. One day, while Churchill was taking a leisurely bath, he was informed that a gang of desperadoes, led by one Peter the Painter, whose real name was Peter Jacobs, had been trapped in a house in Sidney Street, London. Peter the Painter was later identified with the Bolshevists. He had, on this occasion, broken into a jeweler's shop and shot and killed three policemen in making his escape. London police are, normally, unarmed.

Churchill dressed quickly and rushed down to the scene. He found the tenement in which the gang had taken refuge surrounded by the police. The gangsters were keeping up a steady fire from doors and windows. One policeman was shot shortly after Churchill arrived.

Winston had chosen strange clothing with which to round up a gang of criminals. He was wearing a silk top hat and an opera cape. Crouching back in a doorway, with bullets flying inches from his head, he directed the siege of the house. A squad of the Scots Guards were called out to aid the police in what became known as the Battle of Sidney Street. The house in which the criminals were hiding caught fire, and then a remarkable event took place. The London fire brigade arrived to put out the fire.

The police explained that there were criminals in the house and the firemen would be shot at if they stepped into the open. The firemen replied that whether they were shot at or not was beside the point. They were firemen and it was their job to put out fires.

Matters got so hot between the firemen and the police that Churchill had to intervene and rule that, for the time being at least, this was one fire that the firemen had better ignore.

Eventually the building burned down completely. But Peter the Painter escaped. Churchill heard no more of him, though he had plently of trouble in later years with the Bolshevists and Communists with whom Peter the Painter was associated.

CHAPTER

14

FOR SOME YEARS in the early 1900's Germany had presented a growing menace in Europe. Kaiser William II had embarked upon a program of rearmament such as the world had rarely seen before. The German army engaged in massive maneuvers. Churchill was invited to witness one of them, and came away worried at the efficiency and equipment of the Kaiser's soldiers. The German navy was expanded so much that in 1912 it was the equal of the British North Sea Fleet.

It was plain that Germany was preparing for war. Churchill warned his fellow members in the Cabinet of Germany's plans and of what Britain should do to counteract them.

He drew up a memorandum for the Committee of Imperial Defense, in which he outlined what would happen if Germany went to war against Britain and

France. British official opinion was that in the event of attack, France would be able to counterattack by two weeks after the start of the war.

Churchill in his memorandum said that was wishful thinking. The French would be driven back, he said, and the earliest they could counterattack would be forty days from the start of the war. By that time, the ports of France facing England across the English Channel might well be in the hands of the Germans.

Churchill believed that Britain's greatest strength lay in her navy. He was so insistent upon building up the navy that eventually he was given the post of First Lord of the Admiralty.

The British navy has rarely experienced such a hurricane as was loosed upon its top brass when Churchill became head of the Admiralty.

The first thing he did was get in touch with Lord Fisher. Fisher was a professional navy man whose progressive views had made him unpopular and he was now retired. But Churchill called on him for advice in redesigning the British navy. In the weeks that followed, admirals were scattered like bowling pins as Churchill and Fisher revamped the Admiralty.

"Faster ships, bigger guns, more of both and plenty of supplies." That was Churchill's program for the navy on the eve of World War I.

British ships at that time burned coal from the

Welsh mines. Churchill and Fisher realized that oil was a far better fuel, easier to carry and more efficient. They set about getting control of the Anglo-Persian oilfields to supply fuel for the British navy. It has been said of World War I that the allies floated to victory on a sea of oil. Churchill and Fisher provided that sea of oil before the war broke out.

Winston changed the weight of guns on all new British battleships from the old 13.5-inch to 15-inch. The new British battlewagons could outfire any ship in the German Navy.

"What would I do if war broke out with Germany tomorrow?" That was a question Churchill asked himself daily as First Lord of the Admiralty.

One of his answers was to create a division of fast battleships which could get to a scene of action in record time.

Aviation fascinated him. He saw the airplane not as a mechanical curiosity which could travel somewhat uncertainly through the air. To Churchill, the airplane was a potential war weapon which could be used for scouting. So, with Fisher, he created an air arm for the Royal Navy and in doing so helped to bring into being what was to become later the Royal Air Force.

Not all of this was office and conference work. Churchill was never the man to be content with paper work and paper decisions. He liked to get into the practical side of things. So he frequently took flights in the wire, bamboo and canvas crates which constituted the airplanes of those days, and invited other cabinet ministers to join him. Mostly they politely refused.

One man who said he would join Churchill in a "spin" arrived late on the flying field.

"What delayed you?" Churchill growled, for he was anxious to be off.

"I was making my will," his guest replied seriously.

All these reforms and innovations made Churchill unpopular with the older and more conservative naval men. But Winston was ruthless. He could see the coming storm clearly and to be ready for it he would have sacrificed his best friend; for Britain's survival was topmost in his mind.

Then came the day when Churchill ordered the fleet to assemble at Spithead, between the Isle of Wight and the South Coast of England in the English Channel, in readiness for war. This was a tremendous piece of daring, for such an order normally required the consent of the Cabinet. But Churchill believed that the Cabinet, clinging to hopes of peace, would refuse him. So he did not consult them. The whole fleet had hardly been assembled before the storm clouds broke.

On August 3, 1914, Germany formally declared war on France. On August 4, the German army crossed into

Belgium. A few hours later Britain declared war on Germany.

And, thanks to Winston Churchill, the British fleet was ready.

With the outbreak of World War I, two tasks immediately fell to Churchill as First Lord of the Admiralty. One was to convoy the British Expeditionary Force over to France as fast as possible. This job was achieved in quick time without the loss of a single man.

The second task was to blockade Germany by sea and keep the German fleet bottled up. The strategy of blocking has been one which Great Britain has applied to all major countries with which she has been at war. It was applied against Napoleon's France with the same rigor that it was applied against the Kaiser's Germany. The success of a blockade depends upon the vigor with which it is enforced and the length of time which it can be sustained. Time is the ally of the blockaders, and the British fleet was ready to blockade Germany year after year until the enemy's war supplies and food supplies were exhausted.

But this was a waiting game, and one for which Churchill was not suited by temperament. His leaping imagination cast about for ways of bringing the war swiftly and forcibly to a close.

One of these ideas was a giant steam troop-crusher.

It never got as far as being put on a drafting board, for all who heard of it assured each other that Churchill had gone stark raving mad. The basic proposal was to build a kind of heavy roller, operated by steam, which could rumble over the enemy trenches and destroy them and their occupants.

When this idea was turned down, Churchill immediately got busy with another. He asked, why not build landships, armored like battleships and carrying guns? These, if mounted on caterpillar tracks, could break gaps in the enemy lines and troops could pour through after them.

Churchill convinced Prime Minister Asquith of the sense of this idea, and a Landships Committee of the Admiralty was formed. It produced one landship—the world's first tank. But then the program was stopped by others of less imagination than Churchill, and it was not until the war had been in progress for two years that the landships, or tanks, went into action.

When they first appeared in Thiepval in 1916, they so terrorized the Germans that they threw away their rifles and fled.

Churchill made several trips to the front himself. As First Lord of the Admiralty, his business was the seas of the world. But Churchill had been a cavalry officer before he ever dreamed of becoming Britain's naval chief. He had the love of an old warhorse for being under fire, and he chose for his first visit the section of the front at Soissons, where the artillery barrages were of the heaviest. Sir John French was in command of the British troops there, while Churchill's old antagonist, Lord Kitchener, was commander in chief in London. Kitchener in the Sudan had tried to prevent Churchill joining his forces. Now the two sat side by side in the Cabinet, the one conducting the war on land, the other the war on sea.

The city of Antwerp, in Belgium, was at the time besieged by the Germans. The British minister there wired that it looked as if the Belgians must surrender the city within a day or two. Antwerp is an important port, and it would be a terrible blow if it fell into German hands.

At a Cabinet meeting, Churchill proposed that he go to Antwerp himself and stiffen up the resistance. The Cabinet was surprised at the idea of a minister, a civilian, going to a besieged city to rouse the fighting spirit of the defenders. But assent to the venture was given, and Churchill set off.

When Winston arrived, rocketing through the streets in a drab-colored automobile, Antwerp was literally crumbling around him. Huge German guns had destroyed fort after fort. The trenches before Antwerp were swept by German mortar and machine-gun fire and the Belgian defenders were in the poorest spirits.

Churchill's car pulled to a screeching stop before the city's principal hotel and Churchill flung out of it, rushed up the steps and plunged into the lobby with outstretched arms as if to gather the whole of Antwerp within them.

Within a few minutes, Churchill had interviewed the Belgian crown prince and the commander of Antwerp. He told them the city must be held, that British reinforcements would arrive soon, and that he himself was prepared to take command. Whether command was ever formally granted him or not, Churchill assumed it. The king and queen of the Belgians were about to leave for Ostend. They decided to stay, which heartened the Belgian soldiers. Churchill had formed a brigade of marines as shock troops and these were brought to Antwerp to bolster the defenders. Shortly after, two British divisions, one of infantry and the other of cavalry, arrived.

The Germans were unsure whether Churchill was bringing up a large portion of the British Army to defend the city and perhaps counterattack. One day it had looked as if Antwerp were on the verge of falling. The next, the city was putting up the stoutest resistance. The Germans decided to intensify their assault and the casualties in Antwerp mounted higher and higher by the hour. In the end, even Churchill came to realize that the city could not be held. When Antwerp fell, the Belgian casualties were twenty thousand, fifteen hundred men of Churchill's Naval Division were taken prisoner, and a thousand more were missing.

Churchill, however, by his own fighting spirit and persuasion, had delayed the fall of the city for a vital five days. That was sufficient time for Sir John French to secure the French ports to the west on the English Channel. Had they fallen to the Germans, the British army in France would have been cut off.

This vital gain, however, was not known to the British public at the time, Churchill returned to England to find himself severely criticized in the press. The British and Belgian casualty list was very high, and it was charged that he had needlessly flung lives away. Another charge against him was that he, as a civilian, had no right meddling in military affairs.

Churchill ignored the criticisms. He had another plan with which to win the war, and set to work immediately putting it into effect.

CHAPTER

15

RUSSIA WAS FIGHTING on the side of the allies in World War I, and Turkey on the side of Germany. But Russia was cut off by the facts of geography from Britain and France and compelled to fight on her own front as in World War II. It was plain to Churchill that if the British and French armies could link up with those of Russia, the war would be ended very much sooner. Churchill's mind was already busy on this idea when he returned from the siege of Antwerp to his post in the Admiralty in London.

But meanwhile there were more immediate problems to be tackled. The German Commander, Admiral von Spee, had attacked and defeated a British squadron off the coast of Chile in the South Pacific. The blow had to be avenged.

Churchill, in a swift reshuffle of the Admiralty, made Lord Fisher First Sea Lord to replace Prince Louis of

Battenberg. Fisher, as stated before, was a man who had got into considerable trouble during his naval career because of his advanced ideas and forcible personality. But that personality was just what Churchill needed at the moment. On the presumption that von Spee would round Cape Horn and come back into the Atlantic, Fisher and Churchill sent two fast battle cruisers to the Falkland Islands under full steam to intercept the German admiral.

The two were right in their expectations. Von Spee did round Cape Horn, intent upon attacking the Falkland Islands which were an important coaling station for British vessels. He met an inferior force of five British cruisers and started to shatter them with salvoes from the heavy guns of his cruisers the "Gneisenau," "Leipsig," and "Dresden." Then from round a point came the battle cruisers which had been dispatched by Fisher. Their guns were heavier than those of the German cruisers (due to Churchill's pre-war foresight) and in the battle which ensued, most of the German vessels were sunk.

This was a victory that Churchill badly needed. But it did not do much to save him from public criticism. British seaside towns were being shelled by German ships and submarines were sinking more and more of the British merchant fleet.

"Where is the Navy?" people asked, and put the blame for everything on Churchill.

He, however, was busy with his new plan for linking the armies of Britain, France, and Russia. This involved the forcing of the Dardanelles Straits at the eastern end of the Mediterranean, an assault on the Turkish fortifications at Gallipoli, and the capture of Constantinople. That would open the southern sea route to Russia, would permit the reinforcement of the Armies of the Tsar, and would open to Britain the wheat granaries of southern Russia.

Fisher did not like the idea. He knew the Dardanelles Straits as one of the trickiest passages in the northern hemisphere. But he said nothing against the plan at the time, and Churchill managed to persuade the Prime Minister to go ahead with the scheme. He had an ally in Lord Kitchener, who had been asked by the Russians to send what forces he could to their relief in the Caucasus. He could spare none and suggested a naval attack on the Dardanelles.

The idea was a brilliant one. Had it succeeded, it would have shortened the war by many months, if not years. But it did not succeed, and for a simple reason.

Sufficient troops were not sent to make the initial landings on the Gallipoli peninsula. At the time of the attack, there were only a few thousand Turks holding the strategic forts and trenches. By the time Kitchener had got a really large force of men together for the assault the value of surprise had been lost, and the Turks were heavily reinforced.

The second reason for failure was that the Dardanelles Straits had been mined and several troopships were blown up as they inched in toward the landing beaches.

Eventually, what might have been a brilliant stroke, eliminating Turkey from the war and linking the armies of Britain, France and Russia in a huge net surrounding Germany, turned into a prolonged and bloody slaughter.

The work of organizing the army part of the venture was so badly done that troops bound for the Dardanelles had to disembark at Alexandria in Egypt until their stores were sorted. The Turks meanwhile used the time to put barbed wire under the sea on the landing beaches. They built machine-gun nests covering every spot where a landing might be made. When the British, Australian and New Zealand soldiers leaped out of their assault craft to "hit the beach," they were caught in the barbed wire and cut to ribbons by machine gun fire.

The failure of the Dardanelles campaign finished Churchill's career in the Admiralty. In war, success alone counts, and few survive a mistake. Churchill did not survive the bungling of the Dardanelles expedition, though the fault was not his.

Angry Conservatives demanded that a coalition be formed. That is to say, party differences were to be put aside and a government consisting of both Conservatives and Liberals established. Conservatives, they said, must be admitted to the war Cabinet. Churchill was a prime target for their anger, for the Conservatives had not forgiven him for deserting the party. When Prime Minister Asquith acceded to Conservative demands and formed a coalition government, Churchill was removed from the Admiralty. He could have remained in the Cabinet in the curious post of Chancellor of the Duchy of Lancaster—a holdover from medieval times. He did in fact remain for a while, hoping that his counsel would be heeded.

But when after some weeks he found he could do no good continuing as a member of the Cabinet, he resigned and asked for a commission in the army. His request was granted.

Churchill's career as an army officer in World War I—the fourth war in which he had sought active service—was not distinguished by any great victories. That was not his fault. He was anxious to get to grips with the enemy and originally pressed for the command of a brigade.

But the Prime Minister was afraid that if Winston

Churchill were given a brigade, the next that would be heard of him would be that he was marching on Berlin at the head of it. So Winston was given command of the Sixth Royal Scots Fusiliers and the rank of colonel.

He had his adventures, however. Once, told to meet a higher officer at a certain crossroads, he waited there for an hour in driving rain without the officer turning up. Growling, Churchill slithered and stumbled back in the dark to his dugout in the trenches. When he got there he found that the dugout had suffered a direct hit, and the officer who had been its sole occupant at the time had been killed.

Churchill, who had been angry that the appointment was not kept, now saw the affair in another light. He began to wonder whether he was not being preserved by some higher power for a greater task. He had missed death by inches in Afghanistan, the Sudan, in South Africa, and now in Flanders. From that time on, the belief grew in him that a greater destiny lay ahead, and he had but to bide his time to achieve it. This belief eventually grew to become a conviction which could not be shaken. No harm would come to him, he was sure, until he had accomplished some great task which lay in the years ahead.

The Scots Fusiliers, when Churchill commanded them, were holding a portion of the western front at Ploegsteert in Flanders and were under constant enemy fire. Churchill by this time was used to enemy fire but he could not get used to the lice with which the trenches were infested.

One day he called all the officers of his command who were off duty before him.

"Gentlemen," he said, "in addition to the war against Germany, I wish as your commanding officer to declare another war."

The officers looked at each other with surprise.

"I wish to declare war against lice," Churchill went on. "If we attack the lice with the same vigor with which we attack the Germans, I have no doubt but that we shall win."

In the long weeks of trench warfare, Churchill was frequently out by himself inspecting observation posts and sentry posts.

He rarely bothered to pass along the trenches but would walk along the top, ignoring enemy snipers and machine guns. Once a group of highly placed officers paid him a visit. Some of them were desk-generals, who dealt with the paper work of war but knew little of the actual fighting.

"Would you like some entertainment, gentlemen?" Churchill asked.

The officers, with their thoughts on a musical evening, said eagerly that they would.

"Then follow me," said Churchill, and took them for a walk along the top of the trenches.

One of the officers, after containing his anxiety as long as he could, said to Churchill, "Isn't this a rather dangerous way of getting about?"

To this Churchill replied, "No doubt. But then, it's a rather dangerous war."

In his periods of leave from the front lines, Churchill worked on a paper titled "Variants of the Offensive" for the use of General Headquarters and the Committee of Imperial Defense. In it he advocated three main points—the use of body armor to cut down casualties, the use of tanks to launch an offensive and break the stagnation of trench warfare, and the value of surprise in any attack made. The latter was important. Trench warfare had deteriorated to the point that neither side could surprise the other with an attack. The infantry went over the top only after a prolonged artillery bombardment had advertised for hours or days the place they were going to try to capture. The attacking troops were always expected and usually rebuffed with heavy casualties.

Churchill worked on "Variants of the Offensive" in his rest headquarters, situated in a convent to the rear of the lines. One day the Germans decided to shell the convent, and Churchill, working on his papers, was obliged to get down in the cellar. The convent was re-

duced to rubble, but Churchill went back to where he
had been working and picked up his papers. To his
horror he found that the page in his report giving all
the details of the tanks, then a secret weapon, was missing.

Had spies been watching him and seized the valuable paper during the bombardment? Had the bombardment of the convent been started as a means of
getting hold of it? These were the thoughts that flashed
through his mind. Why was only the one page, dealing
with tanks, missing?

Churchill put his hand in his pocket, felt a piece of
paper there, and pulled it out. It was the missing page.
Even in the fury of the bombardment, the importance
of that particular page had been so deeply burned in
his mind that he unconsciously picked it up before
making for shelter.

Churchill had been promised command of a brigade
by Sir John French when he had learned the art of
trench warfare. But before the promise could be made
good, two events interfered with its fulfillment. The
first was that Sir John was replaced by Sir Douglas
Haig. The second, that Churchill was needed in London to make an address to Parliament on Navy matters.

Churchill said good-bye to his command, which had
come to love him for his personal courage and many

eccentricities. One of these included wearing a bright blue French helmet instead of the British tin hat when at the front. Another was the design of a tin tub (part of his warfare on lice) in which he took baths. He presented a strange sight when bathing. It was Churchill's custom to have his batman (or soldier-servant) play records on a squeaky phonograph which stood on an empty beer-barrel nearby. Meanwhile, he luxuriated in the hot water with a cigar in his mouth, a volume of verse in his hands, and, quite often, if a bombardment were taking place at the time, his blue French helmet upon his head. Churchill was generous with his bathtub and sent it to other officers for their use upon request. The only stipulation was that bullet holes were to be carefully patched and, whatever the difficulties with the Germans, the bathtub was always to be returned to him.

Back in London, it would have been diplomatic of Churchill to have trod lightly in his address to Parliament on the Navy. He had many enemies in the Navy, and certainly the Conservatives were after his scalp. It would not be prudent to annoy either of these two hostile groups.

But Winston threw prudence aside. He sailed right into the Admiralty with all his broadsides booming, and his address constituted, in effect, a demand for the removal of several admirals and the recall of Fisher,

who had retired over the ill-fated Dardanelles campaign.

Churchill didn't stop there. He next leveled his guns
on the War Office, which was insisting that there was
a manpower shortage. Too many bureaucrats who
should be fighting in the trenches were employed in
government departments and should be combed out.
That was the War Office view.

Churchill knew that the chief offender was the War
Office itself.

"Physician, comb thyself," he roared to the War Office spokesman in the House of Commons. Then he
launched into an attack on the Somme offensive in
which great losses of life were being sustained for the
gain of a few yards of ground. Why not use new weapons? Why not use surprise? Why sacrifice wave after
wave of infantry on barbed wire entanglements swept
by German machine gunners?

These addresses produced little result other than to
make Churchill more unpopular than ever. But his ob-
jective was not popularity but the winning of the war,
and he refused to retreat an inch from his beliefs.

While he was in London, Churchill's command, the
Sixth Scots Fusiliers, were divided up among other
units and he was now an unemployed colonel and a
member of Parliament.

He had few friends to support him in these dark

days, but he had one weapon denied to men in more powerful positions. That was his command of the English language. He started to write and talk furiously, pointing out the errors of the war and what should be done to correct them. Whatever people might think of his views, Churchill had actual fighting experience on the western front and was entitled to attention.

At this time the allied armies were stretched in a line from the Belgian coast to the borders of Switzerland. The Germans faced them in a similar line. All that was accomplished was slaughter on a scale which the world did not witness even in World War II.

Churchill wanted to break this stalemate whose only result was butchery and denounced the massacre on the Somme at every opportunity.

Eventually the stalemate in the war brought about the downfall of Asquith as Prime Minister. David Lloyd George succeeded him, and Lloyd George was able to give Churchill a place in the cabinet as Minister of Munitions.

There his job was to increase the output of ammunition of all kinds. Waste of manpower or materials he refused to tolerate. He not only took it upon himself to see that the munitions were made, but also to see that they were being delivered and used. So Churchill set up a working day whereby he spent most of the morning in his office in London and a great part of the afternoon at the front with the armies in France. He would leave London after lunch, drive to Hendon, a nearby airport, and be flown to France in a private plane where he conferred with the commanders at the front. Quite often he went up to the firing lines. Nothing could keep Churchill out of shellfire if there was any in the neighborhood.

Once he took George Clemenceau, the aged French Premier, on the tour of the front. Clemenceau was of a disposition to match Churchill's and was known as "The Tiger." The two stumbled along in the trenches, with shells screeching overhead and mortars clumping around them.

"How did you like it?" Churchill asked Clemenceau when they returned from their trip.

"What a delicious moment," replied the French Premier, and the two grinned at each other like schoolboys back from a lark.

Churchill has always loved a brave man, and held that prime ministers should, in war, share the perils of private soldiers whenever the occasion demanded. During the worst days in World War II, when the British army had been evacuated from Dunkirk and Britain was expecting to be invaded at any moment, Churchill took a visitor for a walk down Whitehall.

They came to a stout lamppost near Number 10

Downing Street, the official residence of the Prime Minister, and Churchill stopped to examine it.

"What is it?" his visitor asked.

"That is the post I am going to do my fighting from if Hitler invades," Churchill replied calmly.

CHAPTER

16

ON APRIL 6, 1917, largely as a result of Germany's
policy of ruthless submarine warfare, the United
States entered World War I on the side of the Allies.
To Winston Churchill fell much of the job of equip-
ing the American troops, and he did so well at the task
that General Pershing awarded him the Distinguished
Service Medal. Churchill was the only Englishman up
to that time to receive this decoration.

Meanwhile, the War Office had finally got around to
using the tanks in masses in the way Churchill proposed in his paper "Variants of the Offensive." With
the arrival of the American reinforcements and the use
of Churchill's weapons to break the German lines of
trenches, the end of the war was in sight. It came with
the signing of an Armistice on November 11, 1918.

Britain indulged in a riot of triumph after her long
struggle, and demands for disarmament immediately

followed. But Churchill was not deceived by the peace which ended World War I. He did not share the popular belief that the last great war in the history of the world had been fought. Looking ahead he could see, even at that time, that another European war was possible. So Churchill ordered that all the heavy and medium artillery, for which there was now no use, be put into storage. These weapons, even though outdated, constituted the greater part of the artillery in Britain after the evacuation of Dunkirk in World War II.

Churchill at the close of the war had to some extent cleared his name for the misfiring of the Dardanelles campaign which had brought about his downfall from the Admiralty. A Committee of Inquiry had been held into the Dardanelles expedition which pointed to the bungling of all the plans for which Churchill had been blamed. When the report of the commission was being debated, Churchill said staunchly, "Your commission may condemn the men who tried to force the Dardanelles, but your children will keep their condemnation for all who did not rally to their aid."

History has borne him out, and the whole expedition is acknowledged as a plan of genius bungled by average minds and wills.

Churchill's great friend in the government was the man against whom he had made his first address in

Parliament—David Lloyd George, now Prime Minister. Lloyd George had great admiration for Churchill, and while the crowds of London celebrated the victory, the two sat together at Number 10 Downing Street to discuss the future.

Churchill feared that the Bolshevism which had swallowed Russia during the war might swallow a hungry and defeated Germany with the coming of peace. He proposed that ten shiploads of food be sent from Britian to Hamburg to feed the Germans—Britain's enemy of only a few days before. But Lloyd George counselled that the public hatred of Germany and all things German would not allow such a move. Poison gas, the bombing of open cities, and the sinking of unarmed passenger ships had turned Britain against Germany so completely that the great cry was to hang the Kaiser. Churchill reluctantly abandoned the plan for German relief.

Lloyd George, however, appointed him Secretary for War and Secretary for Air. There was much to be done in demobilizing the massive army with which Britain ended the first world struggle, and Churchill was obviously the man to attend to the job quickly and efficiently.

It was not a job to be handled in a haphazard fashion. The issue of a blanket order for return to civilian duty would throw four million men on the labor market and leave Britain without an army. Everybody wanted out. Added to this, the civil war in Russia still raged. Churchill wanted to help the White Russians, as those loyal to the Tsar were called, against the Red Russians led by Lenin. He saw in the rise of Communism in Russia a new menace to the Western World and spoke out strongly against it.

But he got very little support. Two years after the close of World War I, Churchill wrote to Lloyd George, "Since the Armistice my policy would have been 'Peace with the German people, war on the Bolshevik tyranny.' Willingly or unavoidably, you have followed something very near the reverse. . . . We are now face to face with the results. . . . Russia has gone into ruin. What is left of her is the power of these deadly snakes [the Bolsheviks]."

Churchill's warning of the need for helping Germany and fighting the Bolsheviks, which might have changed the history of the world in the years that followed, were ignored. Germany, left to shift for itself and bereft of many necessities, turned to National Socialism and Hitler for its salvation. Russian Bolshevism which Churchill said should be stamped out by force of arms, turned into Communism to plague the world after World War II.

With the job of demobilizing Britain's huge army completed, Lloyd George next appointed Churchill

Secretary for the Colonies. There was plenty of trouble brewing within the British Empire. In the Middle East, all was in ferment. The Arabs, who had been united on the side of Britain and her allies by the fabulous Lawrence of Arabia, were in a state of revolt. Wartime promises made to secure Arab help in the capture of Damascus, held by the Turks, had been cynically ignored. Emir Feisal, who had been installed as ruler of Damascus, had been ejected by the French.

There had been an armed uprising against the Allies in Iraq, and Palestine and Egypt were powder kegs of discontent, awaiting only a spark to set them off.

Churchill decided to go to the seat of the trouble in the Near East. The mission was so dangerous that he was assigned a personal bodyguard, Inspector Walter H. Thompson of Scotland Yard, to protect his life. Winston took another man along with him—Lawrence of Arabia, the Englishman who had lived for years with the Arabs during the war, wore their clothing and had been completely accepted by them. The two made a perfect team—both were brave men, men of wide imagination and daring, and men with a high sense of honor.

As a result of this mission, the troubles in the Middle East were settled. Emir Feisal was placed on the throne of Iraq as king, it was recommended that a national homeland for the Jews be created in Palestine (though this took many years to achieve), and British troops were withdrawn from Iraq. The troops had been there to patrol and maintain order. Churchill proposed that much of the work be done by airplanes which resulted in a saving to Britain of millions of pounds a year.

Back in England, Churchill turned his attention to Ireland. There, the desire of the people of Southern Ireland for complete independence from Britain had erupted in a reign of terror. Sinn Feiners, who stood for independence, battled the Black and Tans, British troops sent over to suppress the uprising. Running battles took place in the streets of all the principal cities. The author recalls as a child that a mattress was put up against the front door of his house in Ireland to prevent splinters from bullets killing or wounding those inside.

There was great bitterness and much bloodshed on both sides. A conference was arranged in London between Michael Collins and Arthur Griffith, leaders of the Sinn Fein, and the heads of the British government. Churchill did much to smooth matters over.

At one critical meeting, Michael Collins bitterly reproached the British because they had hunted him night and day like an animal with a price of $20,000 on his head, dead or alive. Churchill went to the wall of his study and took down a framed notice.

"What are you grumbling about?" he asked.

"Twenty thousand dollars was a good price. Why, they only offered twenty-five pounds for me." He showed Collins a copy of the notice which the Boers had circulated offering twenty-five pounds for him, dead or alive, after he had escaped from prison camp. Collins' anger turned to laughter and from that moment on a better mood was established which resulted in a treaty of peace being signed between Southern Ireland and Britain.

Eventually, however, the Lloyd George coalition government fell. Churchill had again to face election to Parliament, contesting a seat in Dundee, Scotland. The general election came at the worst time for him. Three days before the campaign opened, he was stricken with appendicitis and had to be rushed off to hospital for an operation. When he got out of hospital, he had only two days in which to campaign. Even so he could appear on the platform only in an invalid chair and was in continual pain. The audience was hostile to him, for the voters of Dundee at the time were very radical. The failure of the Dardanelles campaign was hurled in his face and when the votes were counted, Churchill had lost the election, and was without a seat in Parliament.

But he was not downhearted. He said cheerfully that he found himself without a seat, without a party, without an office—and without an appendix.

CHAPTER

17

WINSTON CHURCHILL, following his defeat in Dundee in the general election of 1922, entered upon a period of political frustration. Largely, this was a result of the changing times. After the first World War, the Liberal Party, to which Churchill belonged, began to crumble away. Its place was taken by the Labor Party which had its greatest strength in the trade union movement.

Churchill was not a trade unionist nor a working man. He opposed the Labor Party and Socialism with which it was identified. He had started in politics as a Conservative. But after he left the Conservative Party, many of its influential members did not want him back. So he really had no party to which to belong. He met this problem by going to the south of France to paint pictures, and then returned to England to write books.

Churchill's paintings are acknowledged by professional artists to be remarkably good. Indeed, he sold four of them in France under the name of Charles Morin for one hundred and twenty dollars each. It was typical of the man that he wanted his pictures sold for their worth as painting, and not because they were done by a famous man. He found a great deal of pleasure in painting outdoors, in the open country. The sense of creation excited him.

Back in England, he continued to write. He had written books on the Malakand Field Force when he fought the Afghans on the Northwest Frontier, on the war in the Sudan when he fought the Fuzzie Wuzzies, on the Boer War, and he also wrote a biography of his father. Now he set himself to the task of writing four or five books about the first World War which were to be called *The World Crisis.*

His writing methods would frighten many another professional author. There was no sitting in front of a typewriter for Winston Churchill. He hired a team of secretaries and having laid in a large stock of cigars, strode up and down his study dictating to them. He dictated so fast that his secretaries were frequently worn out with the work, and left to find easier employment.

Churchill, at one time, solved this problem by buying a dictating machine, and was delighted with it.

On the first day, he had dictated a whole chapter

into the machine and called his family to listen to the results. But when the contraption was turned on, all that came out of it was a series of twitterings, as if a parliament of mice were having a stormy session. Churchill threw the machine away and hired another batch of secretaries.

Often while he was writing he would be distracted by his children playing in the garden. If the play sounded exciting, he would dismiss his secretary and join in the fun.

The first volume of *The World Crisis* appeared in April, 1923, and the second in the following October. The two books made an immediate sensation. They were so clearly written, and with such force and insight, that they were best-sellers overnight. With the proceeds, amounting to eighty thousand dollars, Churchill bought a country house, Chartwell Manor, at Westerham, Kent, not far from London.

His house and writing interested him for a while. He decided to add a swimming pool to his house in which the water would be heated in a shallow basin by the sun. It was a good idea but the sun in England is not always obliging, and Winston had to help it out with artificial heat to get the water to a reasonable temperature. The bottom of the swimming pool was very uneven, for Churchill had decided to do the excavation and put in the cement lining himself. This much can be said for it—there is no other swimming pool like Winston Churchill's in England.

Despite all these activities, Churchill's mind kept reverting to politics. He itched to be back in the political battle again. A seat fell vacant in West Leicester and Churchill decided to contest it.

But to what party could he claim to belong? He had no use for the Labor Party, and many Conservatives had no use for him. He set up a party of his own— Liberal Free Trade—and entered the fray. Churchill, before and during the campaign, had been so outspoken against Labor and Socialism that mounted and foot police had to be detailed to protect him from the crowds. In one working-class district a brick was flung through the window of his car. But Churchill would not retreat an inch despite the hostilty of the electors. He continued to denounce the Labor Party and Socialism and to warn against the dangers of Communism. When the votes were counted, however, he had lost by four thousand.

Another seat fell vacant, this time in the Abbey Division of Westminster. This is an exotic constituency including Buckingham Palace (the monarch does not vote, but the palace servants do), the Houses of Parliament, part of the London theatrical district, a fashionable residential area, and a slum area.

This time Churchill, still rejected by the Conservatives, contested the seat as an independent anti-Socialist candidate. He had some remarkable supporters. Titled ladies gave teas for domestic servants to solicit their votes and the chorus girls of one of London's most famous theaters, Daly's, sent out his campaign literature between acts. Some Conservative members of Parliament had come over to Winston's side. But despite a ding-dong campaign, Churchill lost again. It looked as though he was never going to succeed in getting a seat in Parliament again.

But Winston had not given up. A few months later a general election was held, and this time Churchill won a seat at Epping. Stanley Baldwin was Prime Minister of the new government, and a few days after the election he announced, to everybody's surprise, that he had appointed Winston Churchill Chancellor of the Exchequer. The Chancellor of the Exchequer is roughly akin to the U.S. Secretary of the Treasury.

It has to be stated that Churchill, in the opinion of most financial experts, did not make a good Chancellor of the Exchequer, though the position had been held by his father. In his boyhood days at school he had had a very poor head for figures. His head for figures had improved as a man but the intricacies of twentieth century economics were beyond his grasp. He was not in touch with trade trends and conditions in the Labor market.

His first budget announced that the price of gold would be restored to the value which it held before the first World War. This meant either the buyers of British goods would have to pay more for them, or that wages would have to be reduced.

The coal mines of Britain had been in a bad way for a long time. German coal was back on the world market and was cheaper. The price of British coal must be cut if it was to compete. And since the only way to cut the price was to pay less to the miners, coal mine owners announced that they were going to reduce wages.

This decision resulted in a strike of the coal miners, and the strike spead until it was general throughout England. Not a train ran, nor a bus, nor a truck. Newspapers were closed down. But the government had anticipated the general strike and called for volunteers to run the railroads and essential services.

They came in droves and the strike was broken. Churchill, during the strike, put out a government newspaper called the *British Gazette* to keep the people informed of developments. He was accused of filling the paper with government propaganda, to which he replied that no sensible man ever hesitated in making a choice between firemen and a fire.

Churchill continued as Chancellor of the Exchequer until 1929. In that year another general election was held, and this time a combination of the old Liberal and new Labor Party was returned to power with Ramsay Macdonald at its head.

Churchill retained his seat as the Conservative member for Epping. But for the next ten years, until the outbreak of World War II, Churchill was purely a private member of Parliament, holding no government office.

He became, indeed, a voice crying in the wilderness, and warning of the second World War. But nobody listened to him until it was too late.

CHAPTER

18

IN 1931 Winston Churchill decided to go to America on a lecture tour. He had spoken out very strongly in Parliament against Indian independence, and had been informed that Indian patriots were after his scalp. Many of the terrorists who would like to see Churchill dead lived in the big American cities. So it was decided that Inspector Thompson of Scotland Yard would be assigned to him as a bodyguard.

In New York, Churchill immediately ran into trouble. He decided to walk along Fifth Avenue to see an old friend of his, Bernard Baruch. On the stroll he forgot that in America automobiles travel on the right hand side of the road, whereas in England they travel on the left. When it came time to cross the street, he carefully looked in the wrong direction for traffic, saw none, and stepped into the road.

One second later there was a screeching of brakes

and Churchill was lying in the road, semi-conscious. He had been hit by a taxicab driven by one Mario Contasina. Each apologized profusely to the other and Churchill was taken to a hospital. At the desk arose the inevitable question of whether he had the money to pay for medical attention.

Bleeding from cuts on the face and chest, Churchill settled the matter in no uncertain terms.

"Young lady," he said, "I am a British statesman and a friend of the King." That got him into the hospital without any more delay. He wrote the story of the accident for an American magazine and, with the fee received, spent a few days in the Bahamas recuperating.

The accident is important because all his adult life Churchill has been convinced that he was being saved from death for some great role which he would have to play. The trooper behind him had been killed in the charge of the 21st Lancers at Omdurman. He had come unhurt out of the battle with the Afghans and unhurt also during the first World War though many who stood beside him were killed. He had survived leaping into a ravine as a boy and drowning in a Swiss lake. Now, hit by a taxicab, he had minor hurts when others might have died.

In eight years the role which he was destined to play, and for which his life was constantly spared, would be clear to him and the rest of the world. But in 1931 no-body even guessed at it.

Churchill's lecture tour took him to most of the major cities of the United States and when he returned to London he decided to undertake a tour of another kind.

Ever since his childhood he had been fascinated by his famous ancestor, the first Duke of Marlborough. Now he decided that he would do a life of Marl-borough, in which he would set out the exact truth of one of England's most famous soldiers. Many family documents and letters were available to Churchill with which to write his book, and he determined to make it the best he had written.

Churchill has never approached any task in a modest manner and his "Life of Marlborough" was no excep-tion. He not only assembled and read the copious private papers available on his famous ancestor, but he hired a research staff to ferret into the historical records of England and get together all the material available on the duke. That still was not enough. He hired military and naval experts to explain in detail the strategy of each battle in which Marlborough fought and give him precise information on the arms and men available on both sides, the details of their food supply, and other matters which are factors in the waging of war. Not yet satisfied, Churchill decided that he must visit the site of every battlefield on the Continent where Marlborough had fought and study the lay of the land; must follow the exact routes taken by Marlborough's Armies and see what geographical difficulties they had to surmount.

He set off on this journey of research accompanied by a Professor Lindemann. The journey took him to Blenheim and then to Munich.

In Munich Churchill made a discovery quite as important as any in his researches into the life of Marlborough. It was that the name of Hitler was on every tongue in Munich and all conversation centered around the National Socialists whom Hitler led and who became known as Nazis.

Churchill was interested and asked endless questions about Hitler and the Nazis. A German who introduced himself seemed to know a great deal of Hitler. His name was Hanfstaengl, and he suggesed that if Churchill so desired, an interview with Hitler might be arranged.

Winston said he would welcome such a meeting. He was genuinely curious about the man and about his organization. But he asked Hanfstaengl why it was that Hitler was so opposed to the Jews. Why be opposed to a man because of his birth which was something that no human being could control?

Hanfstaengl could give no satisfactory reply, but

when he met Churchill the next day, he said that the interview with Hitler was off. Apparently he had repeated Churchill's questions to Hitler, and the latter had become angered at them. So it was that Churchill and Hitler, who were to become the leaders of opposing camps in a life-and-death struggle, missed their one opportunity to meet.

When Churchill returned to London he had done a great deal of thinking about the Nazis, and was very uneasy over them. He had heard a great deal of talk in Germany of war wrongs which must be righted and of British weakness. He believed that any real wrongs which had been done Germany in the spirit of vengeance which followed the first World War should be corrected. But he did not believe that the corrections should be made because Britain had become weak and Germany strong.

Shortly after his return to England, Germany demanded the right to rearm. The British people, utterly tired of war, were in a mood to grant Germany's demands. But Churchill arose in the House of Commons to oppose them.

"Do not believe," he said, "that all Germany is asking for is equal status. All these bands of sturdy Teutonic youths, marching through the streets and roads of Germany . . . are not looking for status. They are looking for weapons. . . . To bring about anything like equality of armaments [between Germany and the nations who fought against her] would be almost to appoint the day for another European war. . . ."

His fellow members of Parliament sighed. Here was Churchill again, they said to each other. Trained as a soldier in his youth, he sees a potential enemy in every shadow. Always warning about wars. Well, let him talk on. The League of Nations will take care of all future wars.

Churchill did continue to talk on. But his words fell on ears deliberately deaf to him.

Two months after this speech, made in January 1933 and containing Churchill's first warning of Germany's plans, Hitler came to power. But British feeling was all for peace. The people were war-weary. The government of Ramsay Macdonald presented a plan by which France would dissolve a large part of its army. Everybody believed that disarmament would make war impossible. Churchill alone realized that while the other countries of Europe were in favor of disarmament, Germany was secretly arming.

Yet, to convince Britain of Germany's secret rearmament, Churchill had to have some facts. He was no longer a member of the British government, so the official figures were not available to him. He decided to get the facts on his own.

At his country residence of Chartwell Manor, he set

up what was almost a private espionage service. He wrote to friends in France in high government positions. He made contacts with people in Berlin who were opposed to Hitler. He had many acquaintances in the British War Office and Foreign Office. These were invited to dinner frequently and pumped for all the information they could disclose. Newspaper correspondents were especially welcome at his home, particularly if they had been in Germany recently.

Painstakingly and piece by piece, Churchill, on his own, assembled the full jigsaw design of German rearmament.

Under the Treaty of Versailles, which had concluded the First World War, Germany had been forbidden to have an air force. Churchill learned that the civil airlines and glider clubs of Nazi Germany were being designed so that they could be converted into an air force almost overnight.

Again he arose in the House of Commons to try to awaken Britain to the growing threat of Hitler. Britain's air force, he said was only the fifth in Europe, but the Germans "with their science and with their factories, with what they call their 'Air Sport' are capable of developing with great rapidity a most powerful air force for all purposes, offensive and defensive, within a very short period of time."

Not much later he told his fellow members of Parliament that the Germans already had a military air force, with all the needed ground installations and flying personnel, which would soon be the equal of that of Britain.

His only reward was to be called a scaremonger and a warmonger. Even when a little later the German Chancellor openly admitted that the German Air Force was now the equivalent of Britain's, nobody but Churchill was seriously alarmed. Britain and Europe generally had entered a period of stupor. It arose out of a hatred of war, and from that hatred, a determination to avoid even any talk of war.

But events were marching swiftly toward the final crisis when sleeping Europe would be awakened by the hammering of a mailed fist upon its door. Italy declared war on Abyssinia and Abyssinia appealed to the League of Nations against the aggressor.

Fifty nations, led by Britain, agreed to apply sanctions against the Italians. A commercial blockade of Italy would be enforced, so that goods needed to carry on the war could not be imported. That would end the conflict.

But the blockade was nothing more than a sham. Each nation found excuses for not being sterner in its enforcement. So long as Italy had oil to keep her factories, her transportation, her ships and her war machine running, she could still fight. And everybody jibed at imposing an oil blockade on Italy. The result was that in a short while Italy not only conquered Abyssinia, but in so doing put an end to the League of Nations as an instrument for preserving the peace of the world.

Then Europe and Britain began to heed the warning about German armament which Churchill had been giving. Rearmament was started in the democratic nations, though only slowly. But talk of war was still unpopular. Nobody but Churchill wanted to mention the word. He alone referred to war and threats of war on every possible occasion. He was derided for his pains and scorned as a prophet of a calamity.

Meanwhile, Hitler had seen from Mussolini's invasion of Abyssinia that nobody was really ready to resist an aggressor.

In March 1936, the German army marched into the demilitarized zone of the Rhineland. Europe trembled but did nothing.

Churchill spoke out again, this time in his full eloquence and wrath.

"The government simply cannot make up their minds, or they cannot get the Prime Minister to make up his mind," he roared in Commons. "So they go on in a strange paradox, decided only to be undecided, resolved to be irresolute, adamant for drift, solid for fluidity, all-powerful to be impotent. So we go on preparing more months and years . . . for the locusts to eat."

In 1938, the German army invaded and annexed Austria. Still nothing effective was done to stop Hitler, though in Britain and France the rate of rearmament was increasing.

Churchill tried again to stimulate the government and the Prime Minister, who was now Neville Chamberlain, into action.

"Now," he cried, "the victors (of World War I) are vanquished and those who threw down their arms in the field (the Germans) and sued for an armistice are striding on to world mastery. . . . Now is the time at last to rouse the nation. Perhaps it is the last time it can be roused with a chance of preventing war, or with a chance of coming through to victory should our efforts to prevent war fail."

His words were wasted.

Chamberlain had a policy which can be summed up in the word *appeasement*. He believed that by giving to Germany what was demanded, Hitler's wants would be satisfied and so war would be averted. He did not believe that Hitler really wanted a world war, but only domination over certain European countries.

Chamberlain in 1938 flew three times to Munich to see Hitler for a conference. Hitler claimed part of Czechoslovakia called Sudetenland whose people, he said, were largely German. These people wanted to be united with Germany according to Hitler, who vowed that he had no interest in the rest of Czechoslovakia.

The request seemed reasonable to Chamberlain and he agreed that the Sudetenland should be annexed by Germany.

Chamberlain returned to England jubilant, announcing that he had achieved "peace with honor" and "peace in our time." He was acclaimed a hero and became enormously popular, so great was the dread of a second World War among the British people.

Only Churchill raised a wrathful voice, and nobody listened to him any more and had not done so for several years.

"One pound was demanded at the pistol point," Churchill cried. "When it was given, two pounds were demanded at the pistol point. Finally the dictator consented to take one pound seventeen shillings and sixpence and the rest in promise of good will for the future."

Six months after Neville Chamberlain returned with Hitler's assurance that he had no ambitions on Czechoslovakia, Nazi storm troopers and tanks crossed the border of the little state and occupied its capital, Prague.

The mailed fist came thundering on the door of

sleeping Europe and Britain and France awoke at last.

Now the policy of appeasement was over. The two nations informed Hitler and the world that if Poland were attacked, they would fight.

On September 1, 1939, Hitler invaded Poland.

On September 3, 1939, Britain and France declared war on Nazi Germany.

Prime Minister Neville Chamberlain, a tragic man who had striven mightily for peace and been inevitably wrong, appointed Churchill First Lord of the Admiralty. A few hours later, captains of British vessels of war all over the world received the jubilant message: "Winnie is back."

CHAPTER

19

CHURCHILL'S FIRST ACT when he took over the post of
First Lord of the Admiralty, which he had held a
quarter of a century before, was to establish the traditional sea blockade of Germany.

But this time, due to the perfection of the submarine, Britain found *herself* blockaded. Merchantmen
carrying essential goods to the British Isles were sunk
by the score by the Nazi wolf packs of submarines
which were already at their posts at sea when the war
commenced.

To meet this menace, another British weapon was
employed—that of the convoy. Merchantmen were
ordered to sail in fleets guarded by ships of the Royal
Navy. But the submarine wolf packs still took their
heavy toll and the oceans of the world were lit at night
by the flaming torches of merchant vessels.

On land, during the first seven months, things were

strangely quiet. The French had erected a huge series of fortifications called the Maginot Line, facing Germany. This line, in which France put all of its faith, was quickly manned. A British Expeditionary Force was sent over to fight with their French and Belgian allies. There were a few skirmishes and a strange brooding quiet, called in the United States "The Phony War."

What was taking place was that Germany and Russia were busy dividing Poland between them. The heroic Polish army fought on two fronts before it collapsed. With the end of Poland came the turn of France and Britain.

On April 8, 1940, Hitler turned his attention to Europe, and as a result of the treachery of Major Quisling, who sold out to the Germans, Norway fell. Norway's fall brought about the end of the government of Neville Chamberlain. The man who had made the mistake of seeking peace among men of evil will was blamed for the Norwegian collapse and for not attacking the Norwegian port of Trondheim in a bold move. He lost the confidence of the House of Commons and tendered his resignation to the king, George VI.

His Majesty knew that there was only one man who could rally and lead the country in time of war. That night he sent for Winston Churchill and asked him whether he would head the government. So Churchill, who had warned his countrymen time and again, without success, of the approaching storm, was now called upon to guide them through it. The destiny for which he felt his life had been constantly preserved lay before him. He embraced it eagerly with all that courage and zest he had always shown when the odds lay heavily against him.

It is not the purpose of this book to write a history of World War II, but only to show the part which Winston Churchill played in achieving victory.

His first speech to the House of Commons as Prime Minister plainly stated the part which he expected the country to play. He said:

"I would say to the House, as I said to those who have joined this government: 'I have nothing to offer but blood, toil, tears and sweat.' We have before us an ordeal of the most grievous kind. We have before us many, many long months of struggle and suffering. You ask 'What is our policy?' I will say, 'It is to wage war by sea, land and air with all our might, and with all the strength that God can give us; to wage war against a monstrous tyranny, never surpassed in the dark lamentable catalogue of human crime.' That is our policy.

"You ask, 'What is our aim?' I can answer in one word: 'Victory!' Victory at all costs, victory in spite of all terror, victory however long and hard the road may be; for without victory there is no survival."

On the day of Churchill's appointment as Prime Minister, the Nazi hordes attacked Holland. The courageous Dutch flooded a great part of their country by dynamiting the dykes which hold out the sea. But the Germans plunged relentlessly on. The Belgian army surrendered under the orders of their king, the Germans drove through the gap dividing the British from their French allies, and every vessel in England which could cross the Channel was sent to the beaches of Dunkirk to evacuate the British Expeditionary Force.

The evacuation of Dunkirk stands out as a heroic deed in which three hundred and fifty thousand men were snatched from death or captivity. But Churchill could never regard it as a victory.

In June of 1940, he minced no words in describing the matter to the House of Commons. He called it "a colossal military disaster," and added, "Wars are not won by evacuations."

Britain now stood alone, facing an overwhelming enemy which had overrun almost the whole of Europe. France could be expected to surrender at any hour. Britain had her men back, but they had few weapons with which to fight. A German invasion across the narrow English Channel was regarded as inevitable. Catastrophic air raids from the immense German air armada were awaited hourly. People walked about the streets of the cities, grim-lipped and quiet, wondering whether this was to be the end of a land which, through all the wars of history, had never been invaded since William the Conqueror landed on its shores in 1066.

Were they to surrender or were they to fight? And if they were to fight, what were they to use for weapons?

On June 4, 1940, Churchill arose in the House of Commons to answer these questions for the British people. He said to a silent House:

"We shall not flag or fail. We shall go on to the end. We shall fight in France, we shall fight on the seas and oceans, we shall fight with growing confidence and growing strength in the air. We shall defend our island, whatever the cost may be. We shall fight on the beaches, we shall fight on the landing-grounds, we shall fight in the fields and in the streets, we shall fight in the hills. We shall never surrender; and even if, which I do not for a moment believe, this island or a large part of it were subjugated and starving, then our empire beyond the seas, armed and guarded by the British Fleet, would carry on the struggle, until, in God's good time, the New World, with all its power and might, steps forth to the rescue and liberation of the Old."

When he had finished, the silence of the House of Commons was shattered by such a roar of cheering as that august chamber had never heard before. People straightened their backs, lifted up their heads, and said to each other, "Let them come."

The defense of Britain was now the major problem. It was divided into two parts. First came defense against German mass air attacks. This task fell to the Royal Air Force and the anti-aircraft batteries. Firemen, both professional and volunteers, were mobilized to deal with blazing buildings.

The second part of the defense of Britain lay in repelling a German invasion. The navy, constantly patrolling the channel, would be the first guard against this onslaught. But should the invaders break through the naval patrol, then the task of fighting would evolve on the men of the army and the civilians in their own homes. Churchill thought it highly probable that the Nazis might land in force on the south of England, and expected an enormous slaughter as every foot of ground was fought for to the death.

He had already prepared a slogan for this situation. It was: "You can always take one with you." He organized a civilian army of men over forty to help in the defense of Britain, and gave it the name of the Home Guard.

As Prime Minister, Churchill took into his hands the personal direction of Britain's fight against Nazi Germany. He would give authority to others—but it was authority to carry out his orders. He held the reins of war himself and did the driving.

His working methods were as unorthodox as the ideas which he produced. He would lie in bed half the morning dictating his instructions, and stay up most of the night conferring with his advisers and heads of departments. During the course of the war he issued over a million words of written instructions, all of them models of brevity and often of wit.

The Royal Air Force met the threat of the German air raids, and the Nazis were unable to make a landing in Britain. But Churchill, even in the early days, was not content with a mere defense of Britain. His fighting nature demanded that the enemy be not merely resisted but attacked.

One night, when walking through the blacked-out streets of London, and casting around for a method of hitting back at the Germans, he remembered the Boer commandos who had done so well against a highly trained British army.

Why not form British commandos, who would raid the coasts of Europe, and keep the Germans constantly uncertain of where the next raid would come? The idea had hardly occurred to him before he had decided to act upon it, and so the British commandos came into being.

Again, Churchill proposed that landing vessels made

of steel be designed to take the commandos over to Europe. He devised many kinds of British landing craft which were later developed, and which played a decisive part in the final invasion of Europe.

Even in the days when Britain was fighting alone for her life, Churchill's active and courageous mind was busy with plans for the day when France would be invaded by huge allied armies and the Nazis beaten and driven back to Germany. He knew that all the invasion force would have to be carried from Britain across the Channel to the French coast. And he knew that there were few harbors on the French coast where troops and their thousands of tons of supplies could be landed.

He, therefore, decided that artificial harbors would have to be used, and towed over from Britain. That is what was actually done when Europe was invaded. No field of the operation of war escaped his attention, and when, following Pearl Harbor, the United States also declared war on Nazi Germany, Churchill was present at every major conference in which General Eisenhower and his staff participated.

All this, of course, was behind the scenes. The British people knew nothing of these moves at the time. They saw plenty of Churchill, however, for he made a habit of visiting all the cities which suffered from heavy German air raids, and everywhere he went he was greeted by cheers and cries of "We can take it, Winnie. Let's give them some of it back."

His "V for Victory" sign, made by holding up the first and second fingers of his right hand, became a powerful morale weapon, which Churchill employed constantly.

Quite often the bravery of the ordinary people, whose homes had been suddenly destroyed, and whose relatives had been killed in an air raid, moved Churchill to tears. On a mound of rubble which had once been the hard-won home of a family, a little Union Jack would frequently be placed by the owners—a personal statement of "no surrender." Such sights moved Churchill deeply, and when, in 1941, he went to Canada to confer with the leaders of the Canadian government, he paid special tribute to the people of London.

"Look at the Londoners, the Cockneys, look at what they have stood up to," he cried. "Grim and gay with their cry 'We can take it!' and their wartime mood of 'What's good enough for anybody is good enough for us.' "

Once on a visit to Margate, a British seaside town, he saw an elderly man and his wife standing beside the ruins of their little café. "It was all we had got together in our life's work," the man said, "and now it is gone."

The personal tragedy struck Churchill so strongly

that he gave instructions for a system of war insurance to be started, by which the government would meet all claims for war damage.

Of Churchill during the years of World War II a thousand stories are told. Inspector Walter Thompson of Scotland Yard, who had been with him during his visit to America, was once again assigned to protect Churchill. It was a very difficult job, for Churchill is not a man who lends himself easily to protection.

Once, during a heavy air raid on London, he went up on the roof of No. 10 Downing street, glowering down all opposition, to watch the battle. An aide kept coming up to say something but Churchill would rumble at him, and he would retreat, completely cowed. Eventually, one braver than the rest summoned up his courage and, despite growls and glowering looks, approached the Prime Minister.

"Excuse me, sir," he said.

"What is it?" barked Churchill, suspecting that somebody was going to tell him that he was in danger and should go below.

"I wonder if you would mind moving," said the aide, meekly. "You're sitting on the smoke vent and the people below are almost stifling."

Churchill was given an armored car to travel about in, for the Germans had taken to machine-gunning vehicles on English roads. He would have nothing to do with it. Although all those nearest to him pleaded with him to use it, he refused pointblank. Winston chortled with delight when the heavy vehicle, which could do no more than thirty miles an hour, broke down.

Churchill would not be prevented from making trips to cities which had just been bombed although many sections were still blazing and there was great danger from falling buildings. And he exasperated General Eisenhower many times with his demands that he be allowed to go to the front to see things personally when the invasion of Europe was under way.

It was his delight, when there was a particularly heavy air raid on, to clap his strange hat upon his head, pick up a gold-headed walking stick, and go for a stroll to see what was happening. Once, while dining with the King and Queen, a heavy air raid started. After seeing their majesties into a bomb shelter, Churchill stepped outside to enjoy the show. When the King pointed out to him that this was a dangerous proceeding, and that Churchill had better come back inside, all he got from his Prime Minister was an assuring, though respectful, wave of the hand.

Once Inspector Thompson managed to clap a steel helmet on Churchill's head as he was about to take one of his air-raid strolls. Churchill flung it away without a word and went on with his walk, bareheaded.

Eventually, to protect him, it was decided that an

anti-aircraft battery would be stationed at Chequers, the country residence of Britain's Premiers, and also at Churchill's private home, Chartwell Manor. Winston was delighted. It made him feel that he was a soldier again, and he made a practice of inspecting the batteries and seeing that all was in order. He gave instructions that if ever they went into action, he was to be notified immediately—not so he could go down to the air raid shelter, but so he could watch (and perhaps command) the gunners at their work.

In June of 1941, Hitler attacked Russia. Churchill had always been an outspoken foe of Communism and all it stood for. People wondered what would be Churchill's attitude now that Communist Russia and democratic Britain were fighting the same foe. Churchill did not leave them long in doubt.

"No one has been a more consistent opponent of Communism than I have been for the last twenty-five years," he said in a radio broadcast. ". . . We are resolved to destroy Hitler and every vestige of the Nazi regime. . . . Any man or state who fights against Nazidom will have our aid. . . . It follows, therefore, that we shall give whatever help we can to Russia and the Russian people."

Privately, he told a friend that if Hitler invaded Hell, he, Churchill, would put in a few words for the Devil in the House of Commons.

CHAPTER

20

DURING WORLD WAR II a number of meetings took place between Churchill, Stalin and President Roosevelt. Churchill got on well with both the President of the United States and the dictator of Communist Russia, though there were occasional tiffs between them.

One amusing incident occurred at Churchill's first conference with Stalin in August, 1942. Churchill has a great fondness for goldfish. He had a pond stocked with them at Chartwell Manor and knows many of the individual fish by name. He was delighted to find that at the villa assigned to him outside Moscow, there were a number of goldfish in a tank, and assumed that Stalin had put them there specially.

At their first encounter, therefore, Churchill said how pleased he was to find the goldfish in his villa, and thank the Communist dictator for them. Stalin knew nothing about the goldfish, but recovered quickly from his surprise and said that Churchill might have them as a gift. Thereupon Winston pointed out that it would be rather difficult to take them back to England in a bomber.

"In that case," said Stalin through his interpreter, "perhaps the British Prime Minister would like to eat them for breakfast." Churchill was horrified. It was a sharp illustration of the difference between the eastern and western mind, that Stalin could talk of eating pet goldfish.

During their several meetings, Stalin kept demanding a second front—that is, an invasion of Europe to relieve pressure on the Soviet armies. In vain Churchill explained that a second front could not be launched until all the invasion craft, men, artillery and weapons of every kind had been amassed. Stalin would not listen to these arguments. Once he was so insistent on a second front and so belittling of the British war effort that Churchill lost his temper and pounded so hard upon the table that the glasses on it rattled.

Stalin was impressed by the display, and said, through his interpreter, "I don't know what you're saying, but I like your sentiments."

Although Churchill could get along with Stalin as a person, he could never forget that the Russian dictator ruled through a reign of terror. When, at a later conference, Stalin cold-bloodedly proposed that the whole top command of the Nazi army be shot at the end of the war, Churchill was outraged.

Stalin persisted with the proposal and Churchill grew more and more angry.

"I would rather be taken out into that garden and shot myself," he stormed, "than sully my country's honor by such mass murder." Eventually, Churchill left the table rather than hear more of such talk.

Churchill's relations with President Roosevelt were of the warmest, though the two men disagreed on post-war policies. Roosevelt wanted commitments which would involve, in Churchill's view, the break-up of the British Empire. The President was particularly concerned about postwar freedom for India. Churchill is an imperialist—a believer that the British Empire is a good force in the world for law and order, and should not be dissolved. So the two disagreed on this issue, but got along famously in their personal relations.

Churchill's first meeting with Roosevelt was at Placentia Bay in Newfoundland in 1941. It was not his first wartime contact with Roosevelt, however. In January 1941 Roosevelt had sent his advisor, Harry Hopkins, to Churchill with a message of assurance that the United States would help Britain in every way possible. Churchill was deeply touched at this, and had a deep and unshakable affection for the President.

Churchill crossed the Atlantic in the battleship "Prince of Wales" for his first meeting with President Roosevelt. The President was on the United States cruiser "Augusta." It was a stirring sight when the British vessel, in her war camouflage, entered the bay under an escort of two American destroyers. A large fleet of American vessels lay at anchor, seemingly quite gay in contrast to the camouflaged British battleship.

As the "Prince of Wales" passed the "Augusta," a band of the Royal Marines played "The Star Spangled Banner." The band on the "Augusta" replied with "God Save the King." Both nations had come a long way since 1776. It was at this meeting that the peace aims of Britain and the United States were agreed upon and set forth in the Atlantic Charter. The United States was not then at war, but the President could see the writing on the wall.

By Christmas of the same year, Roosevelt and Churchill were together again—this time with Winston as a guest at the White House. The formalities of their earlier meeting aboard the battleships could now be softened a little. Some red-coated British marines were allowed in the White House grounds as part of Churchill's guard. When Harry Hopkins, advisor to the President, saw them he cried, "How the devil did they get in here? The last time we had them around, they burned the place down." According to another story, President Roosevelt dropped in on Churchill and was horrified to find Winston completely undraped, for he had just had a bath. The President apologized and was about to withdraw, but Churchill replied suavely, "The Prime Minister of Great Britain has nothing to hide from the President of the United States."

On this same visit, Churchill went to Palm Beach, Florida, for a short vacation. He is very fond of swimming (that being one of the reasons he built his own swimming pool at Chartwell). Inspector Thompson, who accompanied him, offered to buy Churchill a swimsuit, knowing that he had none.

Churchill replied blandly that the beach along the rear of the house was private, so he would not require a swimsuit.

"But people are likely to spy on you through field glasses," Thompson remonstrated.

"Well," said Churchill, "if they're that curious, whatever they may see serves them right."

While in Florida, Churchill was warned one day that there was a large shark cruising in the water and it would be unsafe to go in. The dorsal fin of the shark was visible some distance off the shore and there was a degree of doubt as to whether the monster was a sandshark (which is harmless) or a flesh eater.

"Probably a sandshark," Churchill said, and went in

boldly. The shark circled around and then swam away. "See," said Churchill delightedly, "I frightened him away with my huge size."

Churchill has always believed in a greater closeness between the British and American peoples. He once told Roosevelt that he would like to see Americans able to come freely to Britain and settle there and trade without losing their own nationality, and he would like the same privilege extended to the British people coming to the United States. He thought some kind of special passport might be worked out for this purpose.

He has always held that the gift of a common language is a priceless treasure for the two nations, and in making a speech at Harvard University he said, "This gift of a common tongue is a priceless inheritance, and it may well some day become the foundation of a common citizenship. I like to think of British and Americans moving freely over each other's wide estates with hardly a sense of being foreigners to one another."

A very great privilege was extended to Churchill when he visited President Roosevelt in December 1941. At that time he was invited to address a joint session of both houses of Congress. He expressed his feeling of belonging to both Britain and America in the words, "I cannot help reflecting that if my father had been an American and my mother British, instead of the other way round, I might have got here on my own."

Churchill has always been very proud of the fact that an ancestor of his on his mother's side was one of Washington's lieutenants. He once told Adlai Stevenson, "My mother was American and my ancestors were officers in Washington's Army. So I am myself an English-speaking union."

Unfortunately the cordiality between Churchill and President Roosevelt waned toward the end of the war over the issue of imperialism. This was a matter upon which the two could not see eye to eye. Roosevelt saw in the British Empire only exploitation of subject peoples. Churchill maintained that the Empire had spread law and order and respect for individual rights to the far corners of the earth. In the final conferences of World War II, when Stalin was present, this difference stood between the two western leaders. Churchill, in discussing plans for the invasion of Europe, pressed for an attack through the eastern Mediterranean, which he believed would bring Turkey into the war on the side of the Allies.

The plan was similar to the Dardanelles scheme which had been the cause of Winston's downfall in World War I. But President Roosevelt suspected that it had a political rather than military motive. So the attack through the eastern Mediterranean never took place. History must judge whether it would have short- ened the war and changed the course of world events.

When finally the invasion of Europe was ready, Churchill tried every means to get in on it. He growled down warnings that as Prime Minister, he must not be killed, and managed to get aboard the destroyer "Kelvin" to see some action himself. On the way over to France, the destroyer passed some German shore batteries.

"Why don't we fire on them?" asked Churchill.

The answer was that if the Germans replied, the Prime Minister might be drowned. But Churchill was insistent.

"Give them a salvo," he demanded. The destroyer's guns hurled their shells into the German shore batteries. To Churchill's intense disappointment, the German gunners did not reply.

He managed to get to the front artillery positions on another visit, and with great glee chalked the words "For Hitler Personally" on a shell, and then fired it himself to the cheers of the gunners.

As the war years wore to a close and the Allied Armies raced through Germany, even the great spirit of Churchill began to tire. He broke down completely and wept without shame when he received news of the death of President Roosevelt. Despite their differences over the role of the British Empire, Churchill loved

Roosevelt deeply. He told Inspector Thompson, "He was a great friend to us all. He gave us immeasurable help. We would surely have gone under. We would have lost the war. Without him and the Americans behind him, surely we would have been smothered. There was just too much." In his grief over the death of Roosevelt, Churchill showed a different spirit from the defiance of 1940 when Britain had stood alone against Nazi Germany. But he spoke from the fullness of his heart.

When Churchill later received the news of the death of Mussolini, shot by anti-Fascists after begging for his life, his comment by contrast was, "Ah, the bloody beast is dead." And when news of Hitler's suicide in Berlin reached him, he said only, "That is the way I should have expected him to have died."

With the end of the war in Europe, Churchill went through roaring crowds to the House of Commons to make a formal statement of the armistice to the members. As he entered the chamber there was a hushed silence. He made his way slowly to his accustomed place from which, for the past six years, he had from time to time given them news good and bad of the war. He struck his familiar stance, and suddenly the whole House roared its approval of his courage and leadership. Members jumped up on benches waving paper and cheering. Churchill nodded his head, the tears rolling down his cheeks, while he waited for the demonstration to subside. Then, in simple terms, he gave them the official news of the end of the war in Europe.

Afterwards, with other members of the House of Commons and the House of Lords, he attended a service of thanksgiving at St. Margaret's Church, nearby. On the way from the Church to Buckingham Palace to be received by the King, he asked Inspector Thompson, who was accompanying him, for a cigar.

To his horror Thompson found that he had left his cigar case behind in the excitement of the day. Thompson was upset, thinking that Winston needed a smoke very badly. But Churchill explained the true situation.

"I must show a cigar," he said. "The Londoners will expect it." A Havana was procured and, for Londoners at least, the war in Europe with its terrible air raids on their city, ended with Winston Churchill standing up in the back of a car and slowly, and with considerable enjoyment, lighting a cigar.

CHAPTER

21

V ICTORY IN EUROPE brought an astounding political defeat for Winston Churchill. The triumph was
followed immediately by the general election in Britain. Churchill entered the campaign with full vigor
and confident of success. He was determined that a
Conservative majority should be returned to Parliament, when he would continue as Prime Minister.

But when the votes were counted, the Labor Party
had secured an enormous majority. Churchill retained
his seat as a member of Parliament, but he was out of
office. He was deeply hurt, though he did not make his
feelings public. The new Prime Minister was Clement
Attlee, leader of the Labor Party and a close associate of
Churchill's as a member of the wartime Cabinet.

Foreigners, especially Americans, were thunder-
struck by this result. But it was not so surprising to the
British people.

Churchill had made a great blunder during the election campaign. He stated that if the Socialists (the Labor Party) were returned, the end result would be the establishment of a Gestapo or Secret Police in Britain. The people of Britain had fought for six years against the Gestapo and all the rest that Hitler represented. It had cost them great loss both of life and property. They strongly resented the statement, even in a political speech, that they would ever either set up or tolerate for one moment a Gestapo of their own. That was one aspect of Churchill's defeat in the general election of 1945.

Another is best summarized in an anecdote given me by a fellow newspaperman who covered the China-Burma-India theater during World War II. His name is Graham Stamford and he worked on the same newspaper as myself.

Stamford related how at one time a group of British soldiers were penetrating cautiously into the jungles of Malaya. Every now and then there would be the high "ping" of a Japanese sniper's rifle and one of them would tumble over, wounded or dead. Yet they could not see the enemy. The men started to waver, not knowing which of them would be hit next. Then one called out with a soldier's humor, as a comrade fell beside him:

"By gum, this is the last time I'll vote Conservative."

The people of Britain could not forget that it was the Conservative Party, under Stanley Baldwin and Neville Chamberlain, which had permitted the rise of Hitler and allowed the nation to drift into World War II.

So the vote was not directed against Churchill personally, but against his party, which had to take the responsibility for so many blunders of the pre-war years.

There was yet another factor. During World War I, the soldiers had been promised by David Lloyd George, then the Prime Minister, that they would be provided on their return to England with "homes fit for heroes to live in."

They found the homes sadly lacking and their own working and living conditions very little improved. After World War II, they believed that by voting for the Labor Party, things might be better.

Churchill, when the results were known, threw himself into a vigorous attack upon the Labor Party and all it stood for—especially the nationalization of industry—with all his old verve and oratory. Now, instead of being the King's First Minister, he was the Leader of His Majesty's Loyal Opposition. He believed in the right of men to rise by their own efforts. He maintained that no obstacle of class or background should be put in a man's way in his attempt to better himself in the world. But he had no use for the concept that major industries such as steel, railroads, coal mines, and shipping should be owned by the state. This was a principal belief of the Socialists.

Churchill attacked the Socialists, then, with all the dash with which he had charged at Omdurman, more than fifty years before. His great delight was to hold them up to ridicule.

"I hope you have all mastered the official Socialist jargon which our masters, as they call themselves, wish us to learn," he told an audience at Cardiff, Wales. "You must not use the word 'poor'; they are described as the 'lower income group.' When it comes to a question of freezing a workman's wages, the Chancellor of the Exchequer speaks of 'arresting increases in personal income.' There is a lovely one about houses and homes. They are in future to be called 'accommodation units.' I don't know how we are going to sing our old song 'Home Sweet Home.' 'Accommodation Unit, Sweet Accommodation Unit, there's no place like our Accommodation Unit.' I hope to live to see the British democracy spit all this rubbish from their lips."

The austerity program of the Socialists, which demanded that Britain live on iron rations and export everything possible to earn money, Churchill called "Strength through Misery."

Sir Stafford Cripps was for a time in charge of rationing in Britain after the war. He decided how much meat, butter, cooking fats, bread, and clothing the British housewife could buy. He was a tall man with a rather cold and precise face. Once, it is stated, that Churchill, catching sight of him leaving the House of Commons, remarked to a friend, "There but for the grace of God, goes God."

On another occasion, Mr. Gaitskill, then Minister of Fuel in the Socialist (or Labor) government, advocated in the House of Commons that people take fewer baths. This, he said, would save fuel, and he added incautiously that he was taking fewer baths himself.

Churchill leaped at the opportunity offered him.

"When Ministers of the Crown speak like this on behalf of His Majesty's Government," he said, "the Prime Minister and his friends have no need to wonder why they are getting increasingly into bad odor. I had even asked myself whether you, Mr. Speaker, would admit the word 'lousy' as a Parliamentary expression in referring to the Administration, provided, of course, it was not intended in a contemptuous sense but purely as one of factual narration."

Churchill was determined that he would once again be the Prime Minister of England, and nothing would shake him from this resolve. Yet he did not devote these years entirely to politics.

In the years 1945 to 1951 he wrote five volumes of his six-volume history of World War II. The output would stagger a writer who devoted all his time to his profession. To be sure, Churchill, as he did when writing his "Life of Marlborough," employed a hive of underlings to look up the details for him. He also employed a squad of secretaries who took dictation from him—for he hates the boredom of putting words down on pages. Quite often his output was eight or nine thousand words a day (roughly one fifth of this book).

He decided to become a dairy farmer and added several hundred acres to his estate at Chartwell, built barns for his cattle and studied scientific dairying. Not yet satisfied, he built several fish ponds and stocked them with carp. As a further release for his energies he started a racing stable, reviving the racing colors of his father and grandfather which were chocolate and pink. His horse, Colonist II, failed to perform in the championship style of its owner, but Churchill was happy in his new role as a racehorse owner.

In his spare time he painted—painted so well that he was praised by Sir John Rothenstein, director of London's famous Tate Gallery.

He journeyed to the south of France on a vacation and appeared on the fashionable beach at Cannes in a pair of scarlet swimming trunks of heroic size. He went to Switzerland where he lived in a house loaned to him by a prominent Swiss banker on the shore of Lake Geneva. The mayor of the local town volunteered to serve Churchill as a butler. Churchill accepted the offer and throughout his stay called the butler "Your Honor."

Gifts poured into him from all parts of the world and in terrifying variety. He received the head of a famous bull, with a white V on its forehead, from Spain. The bullfighter, who had killed it, the famous Manolete, had dedicated the beast to Winston. Jamaica sent him five hundred cigars, the Swiss a clock which would never need winding, the Australians the inevitable kangaroo, and the New Zealanders a kiwi, a wingless bird found only in New Zealand. From Portugal came a hundred gallons of old port and from South Africa an ebony walking stick. Added to these were innumerable honorary degrees bestowed by universities in all parts of the world. All the honors which were heaped upon him by the free peoples of the world did not distract Churchill from his role of statesman, nor blind him to the dangers ahead. Scarcely a year after the close of the second World War, he pointed forcibly to a new hazard facing the free world.

He had gone to Westminster College at Fulton, Missouri, to receive an honorary degree, and chose the opportunity to stress the danger to world peace and freedom posed by Soviet Russia. He said:

"From Stettin in the Baltic to Trieste in the Adriatic an iron curtain has descended across the continent. Behind that line lie all the capitals of the ancient states of Central and Eastern Europe. . . . The Communist parties, which were very small in all these Eastern States of Europe, have been raised to pre-eminence and power far beyond their numbers and are seeking everywhere to obtain totalitarian control. Police government is prevailing in nearly every case, and so far, except in Czechoslovakia, there is no true democracy."

The world has heard a great deal about the Iron Curtain since Churchill first warned the world of its existence.

From 1945 to 1951, Winston Churchill devoted himself to sharp-worded warnings against the evils of Socialism and the evils of Communism.

In 1951, the rebuff which he had received from British voters at the end of World War II was reversed. At the general election of 1950, the Labor Party once more managed to secure a majority, but it was a meagre one, calling for the support of the Liberals. In 1951 another general election was held when the Labor government fell. This time the Conservatives were returned to power.

Winston Churchill was once more Prime Minister of Great Britain.

CHAPTER

22

WINSTON CHURCHILL'S FRIENDS and family believed that since he had reversed his defeat in the general election of 1945, he would remain Prime Minister for just a little while and then retire, turning the premiership over to Anthony Eden, who had been for many years Britain's Foreign Secretary and Winston's close friend. But they had mistaken their man.

Churchill was seventy-five when he became Prime Minister for the second time. He saw ahead of him two enormous tasks. The first was that of restoring Britain's prosperity which had been wrecked during the war. The second was to ensure, as far as he might, the peace of the world for the coming generations.

At home he set about reversing the policy of nationalization which had been followed by Clement Attlee's Labor government. He tried by every means to encourage the growth of business, releasing businessmen and their enterprises from as many restrictions as possible. Abroad, he attended a series of conferences, which would have exhausted a younger man, aimed at strengthening the alliance of Britain, France, and the United States.

He came to the United States twice for conferences, first with President Truman, and then with President Eisenhower who succeeded him. He flew to Bermuda for a further conference with President Eisenhower and Premier Laniel of France.

When in 1953 Sir Anthony Eden fell ill, Churchill, despite his advanced years, took over the duties of the Foreign Office as well as those of Prime Minister.

In war he had pointed out the realities of the situation to his countrymen without mincing words. In peace, he followed the same policy.

"Lands and nations whom we have defeated in war or rescued from subjugation are more solidly sure of earning their living than we," he warned his countrymen, and bid them work as hard for Britain's prosperity as they had fought for Britain's freedom.

The strain of all this activity began to tell, even on his heroic spirit. In 1953 Churchill suffered a stroke which left him partially paralyzed and unable to speak. His friends feared that he would have to spend the rest of his life in a wheelchair, and an admirer sent him one fitted with all kinds of gadgets designed to make

[206]

living in it less tedious. The chair at first fascinated Churchill. He examined with interest every gadget with which it was equipped. Then the thought of spending his life dependent upon mechanical devices angered him. His bulldog face flushed red and he got out of the chair full of wrath and determined to recover. His fighting spirit saw him through. The paralysis left and he regained the use of his voice. He returned immediately to his duties.

Despite this crisis, 1953 was a glorious year in Churchill's life. King George VI had died the previous year, and Elizabeth II was to be crowned Queen of Britain and its Empire and Dominions in June. Churchill had been born under a Queen—Victoria— and the words "God Save the Queen" had a special sentiment for him.

King George had offered Churchill, at the close of World War II, a knighthood as a member of the Order of the Garter. But Churchill had refused the honor following his defeat in the election of that year. He told friends, "How can I accept the Order of the Garter from my sovereign when his people have just given me the Order of the Boot." Now, however, he went to Windsor Castle to receive his knighthood from the young Queen. With only his wife and the Queen's husband, the Duke of Edinburgh present, he knelt on a red cushion before Elizabeth. The Queen took a gold-hilted sword, touched him with it lightly on both shoulders and said, "Arise, Sir Winston Churchill." There were tears on his cheeks as he stood after receiving the accolade.

The Order of the Garter is one of the oldest and certainly the highest order of knighthood in Britain. It was initiated in the fourteenth century by King Edward III. According to the story, the king was dancing with the Countess of Salisbury when her garter fell to the floor. The King silenced the titters with the words "Honi soit qui mal y pense," meaning "Shame on those who think evilly of it." The saying became the motto of the Order which the King established to encourage courtesy and nobility among his young subjects.

A few days after being knighted, Churchill, clad in the blue velvet robes of the Order and bearing the large diamond-encrusted badge of knighthood on his breast, attended the Queen at her coronation. He looked, in the words of Chaucer, "a very perfect, gentle knight."

Churchill was not unconscious of his role as a great warrior-knight in the service of his Queen. Introducing the Queen's broadcast to her people at the close of the Coronation ceremonies, he said, "Let it not be thought the age of chivalry belongs to the past. Here at the summit of our world community is the lady whom we respect because she is our Queen; whom we love because she is herself."

After the Coronation, the rumors of Churchill's retirement increased. Yet he refused to say whether he was going to retire or not. He used to tease Anthony Eden, his obvious successor, by saying, "Cheer up, Tony, while there's death, there's hope."

It was in 1953 that Churchill revisited his old school, Harrow, and achieved greater honors than he had ever dreamed of as a schoolboy. The whole school turned out to cheer him, and all sang the songs which Churchill had piped heartily in the common room as a boy.

To a favorite song of his, the boys of Harrow added another verse. It was:

> ". . . Churchill's name shall win acclaim from
>   each new generation.
> "While in this fight to guard the right our
>   country you defend, sir,
> "Here grim and gay we mean to stay and stick
>   it to the end, sir,"

Leo Avery, whom Churchill had pushed into the swimming pool at Harrow as a boy, was with him. The two grinned at each other and thought of the long years and dark adventures which had brought them back for this reunion.

It was not until April 5, 1955, that Churchill decided to resign his office as Prime Minister. He drove to Buckingham Palace and in simple words tendered his resignation to the Queen, asking to be relieved of his duties as her first minister. He recommended that Anthony Eden be appointed in his place.

So great was Her Majesty's admiration for Churchill that, as a mark of her regard for him, she did not appoint a successor for two days. In that interval, the first of its kind in the modern history of Britain, the nation was without a Prime Minister.

Churchill left No. 10 Downing Street for the last time on April 7, 1955. A vast throng of Londoners were around the building when he emerged. They greeted him with cries of "God bless you, Winnie," "Good old Winnie," and "You gave them what for in your time, Winnie."

Churchill paused for a minute on the steps, his head thrust forward, nodding his thanks. Then he took a cigar from his case, put it to trembling lips, gave his famous V sign and got into his car.

When he arrived at Chartwell Manor, he told the reporters waiting there, "It is always nice to come home."

That, then, is the life of Winston Leonard Spencer Churchill to date. He continues as a member of Parliament, returning to the House of Commons to resume

[210]

his seat in June, 1955. The end of his story may not be written yet. Indeed, in one sense, there will never be an end to his story, for what he has done will live as long as the English language is spoken.

Whatever trials may lie ahead, his countrymen will always remember those words he spoke in the darkest days of World War II.

"We shall never surrender."

Those words aptly summarize his own life.

BIBLIOGRAPHY

There is a large variety of books on Sir Winston Leonard Spencer Churchill in most public libraries of any size in the United States. The greater number of them are written for adult readers and the most valuable, of course, are those written by Sir Winston himself.

It is not unfair to say that almost all Churchill's books—whether dealing with World War I, or World War II, or even the life of his famous ancestor, John Churchill, the first Duke of Marlborough—are autobiographical. Sir Winston has always envisaged world events as swirling around himself, and not without reason. His "Life of Marlborough" might be taken as a prelude to his own life.

I want to take this opportunity to thank Charles Scribner's Sons, New York, and Oldhams Press Ltd., London, for permission to publish brief extracts from Churchill's *A Roving Commission: My Early Life*. Eyre and Spottiswoode Ltd., of London also kindly gave permission, here acknowledged, to quote from *The River War* by Sir Winston Churchill. My thanks also to the firm of Farrar, Straus and Cudahy, New York, and Inspector Walter H. Thompson of Scotland Yard for permission to quote from his book *Assignment: Churchill*.

In addition to these books, the volumes listed below proved especially useful in my researches:

[213]

Winston Churchill: the Biography of a Great Man, by Robert Lewis Taylor (Doubleday and Co. Inc., New York).

Winston Churchill, by George Sencourt (Faber and Faber Ltd., London).

Mr. Churchill, by Philip Guedalla (Reynal and Hitchcock, New York).

Mr. England—The Life Story of Winston Churchill, by Paul Manning and Milton Bronner (The John C. Winston Co., Ltd., Toronto).

Winston Churchill: a Biography, by René Kraus (J. B. Lippincott Co., Phila.).

Churchill, by John Coulter (The Ryerson Press, Toronto, Canada).

Winston Churchill: The Era and the Man, by Virginia Cowles (Harper and Brothers, New York).

A History of England, by G. M. Trevelyan (Longmans, Green and Co., New York).

The World Crisis, by Winston S. Churchill (Charles Scribner's Sons, New York).

The Second World War, by Winston Churchill (Houghton Mifflin Company, Boston).

Sir Winston Churchill—A Self-Portrait, compiled from the sayings and writings of Winston Churchill by Colin R. Coote and P. D. Bunyan (Eyre and Spottiswoode, London).